# Chasing Genius

### Inside the Mind of an Ultramarathoner

Sukant Suki Singh

Copyright © 2020 Suki Singh

ISBN 978-0-6487153-5-1

Suki Singh has asserted his right under the Copyright, Designs and Patents Act 1988 to be identified as the author of this work. The information in this book is based on the author's experiences and opinions. The publisher specifically disclaims responsibility for any adverse consequences, which may result from use of the information contained herein. Permission to use information has been sought by the author. Any breaches will be rectified in further editions of the book.

All rights reserved. No part of this publication may be reproduced, stored in or introduced into a retrieval system, or transmitted in any form, or by any means (electronic, mechanical, photocopying, recording or otherwise) without the prior written permission of the author. Any person who does any unauthorised act in relation to this publication may be liable to criminal prosecution and civil claims for damages. Enquiries should be made through the publisher.

**Design & typesetting:** Busybird Publishing www.busybird.com.au

*For my mum,*
*Thank you for raising me and teaching me some basic life skills like helping others, cooking, respecting women and following my passions and dreams.*

*I love you so much and I will always miss you!*

# Contents

| | |
|---|---|
| Introduction | 1 |
| Delirious West 200 Miler, 2020 | 3 |
| Chasing Humanity | 38 |
| Life is Too Short, So Help Others | 59 |
| Power of Never Giving Up | 72 |
| Power of Resilience | 102 |
| Chasing Art | 138 |
| Chasing Improv Comedy | 156 |
| Giving Back | 173 |

# Introduction

Over the last 31 years of my life, I have been trying to find my purpose. Why did I come to this beautiful world? In 2019, I found my purpose in running ultramarathons, writing books, painting, doing improv comedy and little bit of cooking. I do not claim to be the best runner in the world, but I am trying to live a meaningful life by doing something that helps me build my confidence and makes me feel good about myself. It is something I do to refuel myself once a week.

I believe that taking care of our mental health is very important in this world and, having ran around 22 marathons and few ultramarathons, I have learnt how to become more resilient and tackle pressure to some extent. April 2019 was a very difficult period in my life, and in this book I have shared my experiences of how I recovered from that dark phase by doing something I love the most.

In future, I dream to do lots of runs in order to create a positive impact in the world. I have a vision of creating a sustainable planet where people are using fewer cars and are walking, cycling and running to better our future. I also believe if we change our lifestyle, we all have the ability to make this world a better place and that's why I have also shared my love for the environment in this book.

Running has taught me a lot of life lessons and whenever I have any challenging adventures, I come across some exceptional people who, according to me, are 'chasing genius.' In this book, I am trying to investigate the mind of an ultramarathoner.

This book is an incredible true story of me taking part in one of the most challenging ultramarathons in the world. It is a story of my failure as I was disqualified at 204km mark at the Delirious West 200 Miler challenge in February 2020 in Western Australia, but it is also the success story of some of the best runners in the world who ran this 350km ultramarathon. I have also laid out the lessons I have learnt through my failure and how chasing my other passions like art, improv comedy and practicing acts of kindness have helped me become a good human being and recover from stress and anxiety.

# Delirious West 200 Miler, 2020

### Understanding the Mind of an Ultramarathoner

19 February 2020, in Northcliffe, Western Australia, was a day that some of the best athletes have waited so long for. In this part of the world, at the tip of the Indian Ocean, something very extraordinary was about to happen – it was not every day you get up in the morning and decide to run a 350km ultramarathon in a jungle.

It was the day to fulfill the crazy dreams of around 64 incredible people who decided to test their limits by running a 350km ultramarathon, or 220 miles. It is said that an adventure like this can change your life for good. It is a race so long that some male runners might have to shave in-between. There were four sleep stations and 25 aid stations, where athletes can rest, take showers and refuel themselves. It is almost like running two marathons a day, with a rough distance of 80 to 90km, as there is a strict cut off of 104 hours. A runner is expected to sleep maximum of 4-8 hours in a 104-hour duration. Some even remain without sleep the entire distance, which comprises of mountains, rivers, dense forest, surf coast and all varieties of trails. I would say normal humans on this planet would freak out just hearing about this unique survivor challenge. I am an advocate for the importance of sleep in our lives; it is crucial for our peak performance as athletes, or in order to perform better at work. But a run like this is designed in such a way that we can't afford to sleep much. If we sleep for more than eight hours in this entire 104-hour challenge, we may not be able to finish it under the cut-off limit of 104 hours.

These athletes were truly chasing something else in their lives, which the rest of us are still not sure what to call. In my terms, they were 'chasing genius'; they were redefining the limits of human resilience. They were chasing the third metric of success – which is our wellbeing, mental health and humanity. I came to know about the importance of the third metric after reading Arianna Huffington's book, *Thrive*. Often, we are so busy chasing the two metrics of success, money and power, that we forget the third metric, which is how to live a meaningful life. We live in a world today where stress, anxiety and depression are at all-time highs. This is also the time when we have to find our purpose. The very reason I decided to do this challenge was when I realised that my physical and mental abilities are greater than I ever thought.

So, I decided to test my limits by taking part in one of the most challenging events of my life. I also got to interview some astonishing people on this planet, who were trying to show the world what the mind and body are actually capable of achieving. I believe if we prepare our minds, then anything is possible. At this time in my life,

I was looking for an adventure that could either break me or make me into the best version of myself. So, I Googled, 'toughest ultramarathon in Australia' and I got 'Delirious West 200 Miler' as one of the results. It cost a fortune to register for such a challenge, so my all savings were gone.

I met my running coach, Glenn Monaghan, on a Facebook group for the Delirious West challenge three months prior to the event. I can't tell you how grateful I am to have met Glenn, as he is one of the most experienced runners in the world and has done few Iron Man challenges. We immediately exchanged numbers on Facebook and he guided me on how to train for such an extreme challenge. Glenn had done this challenge in 2019, the debut year of Delirious West, so I listened to his advice very carefully. I got to meet Glenn's beautiful family when he provided me with free accommodation at his house in Perth. I was so glad to meet his beautiful wife, Louise Monaghan, and his three children, Amy, Nicole and Ben. They were one of the sweetest families I met in Australia. While we drove to Northcliffe (the starting point of the race), roughly 350km from Perth in a hired campervan, Glenn shared his running experiences over our four-hour journey. Glenn told me that he, along with his wife, had migrated to Australia many years ago from Ireland and were now contributing to this multicultural nation. I was clearly nervous as a first timer doing a 350km challenge in a jungle. So, Glenn and his family were kind of a lifeline to me.

While we were in the campervan, Glenn told me he did such extreme challenges to test his limits. When I asked him if he thought life was like the trail of an ultramarathon, Glenn said:

> 'Definitely. An event like this prepare[s] me for life. Life is full of ups and downs and every one of us go[es] through the same [things]. Ultramarathons have ups and downs. You learn how to keep going in the low moments. If you can do that in life, it is much better. I believe that these endurance events have made me mentally stronger. Even … when I am not running ultramarathons, the lessons I have learnt so far from these events help me to become the best version of myself every day.'

He then added, 'everybody has challenges in life. Everybody has got same time restrictions. I believe it's how we react when things start going wrong that makes us who we are.'

Talking further about his fitness regime, diet and how he takes time to do such events, apart from working full time in a construction company, Glenn said:

> 'First of all, I don't [have many] excuses in life and I don't have time for people who give excuses. I always tell people that they have the same amount of time as I do. I work twelve hours a day and train one or two hours a day. So, if I can do it, anybody can do it. It's all about really wanting to do something. It's about pushing yourself every day and becoming better. It's about going to [the] gym regularly and eating properly. I have been on a completely plant-based diet since 2016, when I did the Ultraman challenge. I did lots of research and got results that with a vegan diet, recovery is better after such extreme challenges, and since then I have never looked back. Fresh vegetable[s], nuts, spinach, fruits, I try to consume on a regular

basis. Like others, I do have cheat days, but I know very well what is good for our body.'

When I asked Glenn about all the challenges he has had until now, and how they have helped him become a good human being and maybe even helped his relationships, he said:

'When I was thirty, I had my own company and I worked really hard for my company. But I wasn't physically fit, with the kind of work I was doing. So, I decided to do my first marathon at age thirty and I just got hooked. I decided to do the Iron Man triathlon when I turned thirty-one. Till now I have done six Iron Man Triathlon[s] [and] three or four half Iron Man Triathlon[s]. I have been doing this for the last ten years and it has helped me become a person who sets goals for himself. It has also helped me build relationships and bonds with people who do such kinds of challenges and build friendships that last for lifetime. After doing these triathlons for many years, I decided to take a break, and took up ultra-running. I registered for 100 miles. After Ultraman challenge, I knew there were no limits to what the body could do and I had to see how far I can push my mental strength. So, I registered for the 100 mile race with ten weeks of training. When I finished the 100-mile race, someone told me about the 200 mile race. So, Delirious West is my second 200 miler and I have done three 100 miles race so far. Apart from this, I have completed numerous marathons and it's hard for me to count the exact numbers. I work in a very stressful environment and of course such kinds of adventures have helped me enhance my performance at work.

I enjoy the training, I enjoy the challenge, enjoy the people I meet along the way. There are two versions of me: old Glenn and New Glenn. The old Glenn had a wonderful job and family but was still not happy. There was something missing. So, when life becomes too comfortable, we may not be truly happy. That challenge was missing. The new Glenn loves those challenges.'

Finally, Glenn gave me the most important advice for my first attempt at the 200 Miler challenge: to believe that I could do it.

> 'Don't lose that self-belief. You will have lots of ups and downs. The big thing is to never give up unless it is very serious. Keep moving forward, keep smiling and enjoying it as much as possible. Believe it or not, it's hard to feel pain and smile at the same time. There will be times when you will not smile at all. Try your best, keep moving, keep doing what you are doing and bad times will pass. Keep thinking about *why* you are doing it and consider it as a lifetime of adventure within four days.'

It was such a pleasure talking to Glenn – he just boosted my confidence levels. I remember when I told an Uber driver in Melbourne that I was going for this 350km ultramarathon – he scared the hell out of me! He said, 'I will pray you come back alive.' But Glenn's positivity just changed my perspective and I became hopeful that I could do it.

Finally, after a long drive, we reached Northcliffe; a small town located in the lower South West region of Western Australia. It was a very strange place for me. I didn't know anyone in this town, but as all the runners gathered at the Northcliffe hotel for a light dinner and race briefing, I quickly tried to introduce myself to other runners who had come from around the world.

During a quick chat with Sean Nakamura, who is a very experienced ultra-runner and flew from the USA for this event, he told me that it was his first time in Australia and that he was super excited to see some kangaroos.

'It's a very new trail for me. I wish to enjoy the beautiful landscape, and the organiser of this event, Shaun, has been very hospitable to me, so it motivated me to try such an adventure like Delirious West,' Sean said.

'In the last two months, I have been running 100km and 50 miles and regularly training for it.' He told me he would try to finish the challenge in two nights.

Next I came across Stefan Gierczycki from Sydney, who had 25 years of running experience. I am so grateful that he also bought my first book, *Limitless Humans*.

> 'I have never done anything more than 100 miles. This is one of the toughest and longest runs in Australia, and I wanted to do something that not many people have done before. My goal is to reach the end. I expect to finish this challenge in under 100 hours,' he said.
>
> 'I run all the time. I did an extremely challenging event in France called CCC, which is a unique race in the mountains and is one of the most prestigious in the world. I have been lucky enough to get a support crew and a pacer in this 350km challenge. When I am feeling down, they would motivate me and help me reach my goal,' Stefan said, while sipping his last beer for the day.

Talking about his diet, Stephen said he generally prefers seafood and will make sure he eats something at every checkpoint.

> 'I didn't run last year but I saw many people pulling out from the event at 200km. So, my strategy for this adventure is not to go too hard tomorrow (February 19, 2020) in the sun. When you feel like you have got some energy, you pull back,' he added.

Speaking to these athletes made me feel charged and nervous at the same time. A lot of things were going in my mind, like, what if I get lost in the jungle at night? Can you imagine running continuously for 100 hours? In fact, nobody was really sure they would be able to finish this challenge, except for a few who did it a year ago, as well.

Next, I interacted with other runners who were excited and nervous, just like me. I was going to the washroom to relieve myself again and again out of nervousness. I couldn't believe I had finally reached the start line of this mega-adventure.

It was lovely interacting with one of the female athletes from Albany named Charmaine Brown. There were 21 female runners who took part in this challenge. Charmaine did her first 50 miles run in 2019 and this was her first 200 miler.

> 'I am expecting to finish this challenge in 100 to 104 hours. I will try to sleep not more than two hours at each sleep station. I am not going to follow any special diet but will try to eat something at every checkpoint, and some of my friends are here to cheer for me as well,' Miss Brown said.

I met with Dan King next, who attempted this challenge in 2019 as well but did not finish (DNF) and unfortunately pulled out around 250km mark. 'I got injured at around 80 km. The most important advice I would give is not getting lost in the track and using finger socks to prevent blisters,' King said. He thought of coming back in 2020 with better preparation. 'I am expecting to finish this challenge in around 80 hours,' he added.

Dan really had a great personality and I felt confident after listening to his story.

Another female athlete I got to interact with was Jen Millum.

> 'I love running all the time. I have a great support crew and pacers who are going to motivate me at various aid stations. I have done 100 miles before. For this challenge, I would say not getting lost is important by carefully looking at the yellow snake marks along the Bibbulmun Track. And as far as our sleep is concerned, it all depends on how much sleep each runner needs, but at the same time, we have to make sure that we do not miss the cut-off.'

Finally, it was so funny to meet Nick O' Neill, who told me he slept over the snakes in this challenge in 2019. I remember recording this in my phone and posting on my Instagram. How often do you see such courageous people? He actually helped me feel better and I felt confident by listening to his running adventures.

'I finished this challenge in 2019 in 73 hours. It is not a race; it is a survivor challenge.' When I asked him if there was any danger of snakes, he said, 'I slept over one last year. It didn't bother me at all.' He said this laughing out loud.

> 'Some of the best advice for people out there who can't run even 350m is that run when you can, walk when you can, but you have to just keep moving in this challenge and in life,' Nick added.

I would say all of the 64 runners who took part in this challenge had a great story. Having the courage to reach the start line was itself a massive achievement. They were about to do this survivor challenge, which could teach us how to live a meaningful life, how to deal with pressure, stress, anxiety and depression. It could further teach us how to be mentally strong when the world is against us, how to be resilient when we lose a loved one and how to be hopeful in life when there is no hope for our future. Trust me, if we have hope in life, anything is possible, as hope is the most powerful word in the English dictionary. Millions of people live in extreme poverty in this world. They have no roof over their heads, but what they do have is hope that tomorrow will be a better day. Similarly, we 64 runners had hope that we would be able to finish this challenge in under 104 hours.

I got little bit more confident to do this challenge when I met Breeze Sharma, an Indian Navy officer who did this challenge in 2019 in 95 hours and is one of the most experienced ultramarathoners in the world. Some of his achievements include Bad Waters (135 miles in California, which was dubbed by National Geographic as the toughest ultramarathon in the world), UTMB in France, Brazil 135 miles, the 24-hours Treadmill challenge in India and many more.

I finally got to interact with this legend when he arrived in Northcliffe.

> 'I have been running for a very long time. Whenever I register for any event, I start training few months in advance. In order to train for Delirious West, in the last two months I have been running 100 to 120 miles per week.' Breeze said.

When I asked him what his secret was to his powerful running CV, he smiled and said,

> 'There are so many distances involved in ultra-running that start from 42k onwards. Generally, there are 50k, 100k and 100 miles, which many runners can do after proper training. But a race like a 200 miler needs a very different kind of training. Your mindset should be really strong in order to do such a challenge. The execution of your strategy is very important, and most importantly, how to survive in such environment. In these kinds of races, anything can happen. There are dangers of bushfires and snakes, so one has to negotiate with the environment in order to do such extreme adventures. The race is secondary, as one has to learn how to survive in those extreme situations. When the mind is stabilised, then I don't think distance is a matter.
>
> 'When I have these adventures, I deeply connect to nature. I don't think I do such adventures to test my limits or to think I am doing anything extraordinary, but the main point is to learn the art of objectifying the pain, to recognise the pain and divert the mind. These are some of the key points where one can succeed in these kinds of events,' said Breeze.

This was also probably some of the best advice I got until now.

> 'I live in Mumbai and it is a city that never sleeps. There are all kinds of attacks, like the digital revolution, if you talk about the day to day life like the traffic, crowd and all these things are around me. So, my point is that the meaning of life is not there. I have been a professional mountaineer and when I adapt to such kinds of races or adventures, I better understand the meaning of life. Sometimes, I do feel we all have become meaningless in this selfish world. I don't know what we all are

chasing in this world. Very few are chasing their purpose and finding their true meaning.

'By doing such kinds of endurance races, one truly finds the meaning of their life. Otherwise, it's just like living a life like a machine. There are many kinds of power in this world, like political power and money, but if you have intellectual power, mind power, I think the rest of the powers are zero. Because when you run such kinds of ultramarathons, you find your intellectual power. You get a different kind of confidence and courage. You develop leadership quality and personality development. So, if we develop this mental power, then all other kinds of power have simply no meaning,' Breeze added.

Talking further about the trail, which he completed in 2019 in 95 hours, Breeze said that it is marked properly so there are less chances of becoming lost.

'In case you get lost, you download the GFX file and keep checking it and even if you get lost, you wait for someone, and other runners might guide you. I have done research about the snakes and there are five kinds of snakes in this area. Some snakes are not poisonous. In my run last year, I saw so many snakes on the trail in the middle of the day, when the temperature was a bit warmer. There's only a short portion of the trail where you will find snakes. So, there is not much to worry about,' Breeze said, while giving me some advice on my first 200 miler challenge.

'This Delirious West 200 Miler will be my 27$^{th}$ 100 miler plus race. 350km is the maximum I have done in my life. Apart from that, the toughest I have done is UTMB in France,' Breeze concluded while talking about his running CV.

I got so much motivation for this challenge just by listening to stories from Breeze and other runners. The most important thing Breeze said was about mind power and intellectual power. Today, we live in a world where we need people who are mentally strong, and such kinds of events helps us become mentally strong. Some of us often freak out when we don't find our TV remote, and these people are truly chasing some meaning in their lives.

Finally, the day we all waited so long for arrived. It was a day that would go for a very long time, a run that wouldn't finish anytime soon. There was beer drinking with a shoe ceremony at 7am at the starting point. Finally, the race kicked off. I practiced gratitude for all the things I had in my life, prayed for five minutes and started running with 64 other runners. We went in the wrong direction in the beginning, but continued our journey until the Chesapeake Rd (West) aid station.

'Welcome to Jumanji,' I said to myself. Sometimes, we have to know ourselves better, or in other words, self-reflect. Thinking about who we are and what our purpose is in the world is very important. A challenge like this prepares us for life. As I reached the 41.5km mark at Chesapeake Rd (East) I had some cup noodles and drinks to refuel myself. I felt the salt from my body going away. Then came another aid station, named Dog Road, at 53.2km, then Pingerup Rd at 71.2km, then Brooke Inlet Rd at 87.5km, and by this time it was very dark and I took off my black diamond headlights, which had a visibility up to 70 metres. I rested here for a while eating all I could.

I decided to continue running with a runner named Duc Do. I kept meeting this runner again and again at various points. I remember once, late at night, we felt as though we were talking to the stars. I looked over the moon and stars and Duc Do told me, 'Just remember, you decided to do this event so you should know the purpose of such an adventure.'

I started asking myself what my purpose was and I realised that I was doing this adventure to get away from all the dirt in my life. I started thinking of April 2019, when a dark phase struck my life. I wanted to get rid of all the toxic and negative thoughts that ever came into my life. I wanted to get rid of hatred, jealousy and comparison. So, let me go back to April 2019.

It was April 15 2019 when I went to India on a trip. I came back on April 25. On April 26, I was very close to jumping in front of a train. I was sitting at Springvale station, waiting for the train, but I didn't have enough courage to end my life. I went back home shivering that night. I don't know what was going on in my head, but this is just an example that your life can change in 10 days. I was trying to Google medicine for anxiety. To be honest, there is no medicine for anxiety in this world. I had to find the medicine myself – and that was running ultramarathons. I remember calling my friends Nancy and Hui and sharing my problems with them. We met at the Pancake Parlour in Melbourne Central and they were surprised to know that a guy who runs 42km marathons like a joke was saying all of this. I told them exactly what happened in that trip. My relationship with my family had broken down. I was considered the biggest failure in the world by my family; my father was extremely upset with me for making friends with people from other countries, races and religions. So, the anger was there but I didn't know it, and it burst out like a bubble during that trip. Also, in an emotional statement, my father said he might be seeing me for the last time at the airport, when I was coming back. It made me emotional and weak. I was not able to focus on anything for the next few weeks, so I decided to block all my family members from my social media to better focus on my mental health. I started meditating and writing journals in order to find my purpose. My friend gave me a Bible to recover from that bad phase of mine.

I completed my first 100km ultramarathon on September 21, 2019 with the help of my amazing support crew, Nancy and Hui, and wrote my first book *Limitless Humans*. After acquiring a little bit of success from my first book and an appreciation letter from the High Commissioner of India, His Excellency A. Gitesh Sarma, and from the office of the Prime Minister of Australia, Scott Morrison, my dad completely changed. I remember him calling me and saying, 'son, you are a legend.' I am pretty sure every Indian living overseas go through similar challenges in life with their parents or family. My father, who strictly believed in arranged marriages before reading my first book, now gave me freedom to marry the person of my choice. To be honest, my book has nothing to do with marriage – it is all about running – but it did create an impact in his life and many others.

Running became my medicine for stress and anxiety, so I started having all kinds of extreme adventures. This was my purpose: doing the Delirious West to become a good human being, and to become mentally strong. We can't make everyone happy in this world, but we need to be mentally strong and not hold other's opinions too strong in our heads.

The night of February 19 2020 was almost over. I saw some runners sleeping on the rocks. I tried resting for a while just around the Mandalay Beach Rd 109km mark. Later on, I met another runner named James Brougham, who kept meeting me again and again at various points. I remember stopping at some point around 3am and looking up at the stars. At that time, I remembered a quote from Oscar Wilde, who said, 'We are all in the gutter but some of us are looking at the stars.' Imagine if we all started looking at the stars at night to find our meaning and purpose in life. We would be the happiest people in the world.

Later, as the night passed through the deep river crossing, I meditated and kept running for a while. I was able to reach the first sleep station, called Walpole, at 140km mark around 2pm on day two. I rested here for 1.5 hours, took a shower and changed my socks, which were full of dirt. Finally, Glenn's family, who were tracking me on the Delirious race map, met me at the Walpole sleep station. They asked me how I was doing and if I needed anything else. I gave them some stuff to be kept at the next sleep station, since they were driving the caravan. I hugged Louise and took off from this sleep station. It took me two to three hours to reach next aid station, named the Giant Tingle Tree, at the 150km mark. It was a beautiful view and I was surrounded by nature. There was no pollution and no noise, so it was a perfect place to find peace and purpose.

I reached this on day two at around 6pm. I rested here for a while and took some pictures of the Giant Tingle Tree. I was in-between Northcliffe (the starting point) and Albany (the finish line). I also came to know that the boardwalk protecting the Giant Tingle Tree are the largest girthed eucalypts in the world. I came across a signpost which had some great information about the flora and fauna on this native forest in the southern hemisphere. This forest was known as Karri Forest. I was in a very extraordinary place, doing extraordinary trail running. I was loving each and every moment of it, but at the same time, it reminded me of what my running coach, Glenn, had told me; that you have to learn how to smile through the pain. This was a true test of resilience and I was about to reach Tree Top Walk. It was late at night, around midnight, a time when the rest of the world was sleeping while we were chasing genius.

I came across a couple of runners as their headlights sparkled through the forest. They were from Victoria and told me they were taking a break to celebrate running more than 160km. Later on, I followed them, but my speed became progressively worse and I was resting on the trail, taking breaks again and again. Finally, I reached Tree Top walk and I met Shaun, the organiser of the event, who was dressed up in a monkey suit to cheer us up and to give us hope because we had crossed the halfway mark. I was completely drained at this point, so I rested here for an hour. I felt asleep immediately and when Shaun finally woke me up, it was 4am and I was supposed to reach Peaceful Beach Sleep Station by midday on day three. I put my headlights on and went as fast as I could. The trail was not clearly visible to me, so I went the wrong way a couple of times. This time, I didn't come across any runners, so I was all by myself. I was praying every minute, hoping I would reach the sleep station, but this Bibbulmun Track was never-ending. I was coming across the ocean, then the forest, mountains and desert. It was a never-ending track with lots of variety. I seriously thought to myself, out of 7 billion people in this world, how many dare to go on such an adventure?

The track helped me connect to diverse areas of natural beauty and soak in its immense beauty, from the Jarrah forests, to clifftops and surf coasts just above the tip of Southern Ocean. It's not only the different types of flora that made me happy; there were many lakes, rivers and a myriad of mammals, reptiles and birds. After doing some Google searches, I also came to know that I was running at the Southwest Botanical Province, which is one of the world's 34 terrestrial hotspots for conservation. Imagine, after living in such a stressful world today, taking time off to soak in nature's immense beauty. We might forget all our problems. I truly love nature as a runner and as a human being. Nature teaches us beautiful lessons and it also makes us feel good.

It was roughly 11am and the sun was on top of my head. Unfortunately, I ran out of water at this stage and I could see no runners around me. I tried eating some almonds and walnuts, which I had stored in my bag, but with the lack of water the nuts just gave me a dry cough. Out of frustration I just threw the dry fruits packet in the bushes. I was just praying to reach the beach so that I could wash my legs and drink some water. I started thinking, what would British adventurer Bear Grylls do? I tried my best to reach the beach, but I mentally gave up for a while. I started to think that I wouldn't be able to finish this challenge. So, I rested for a while at the coast of Peaceful Bay. It is said that when your mind gives up, one quits in a race or in life. The important thing is to convince the mind that nothing is impossible.

I spent some time drinking water and washing my legs after taking off my shoes. This 10-15 minute break cost me the challenge. I messaged my friend in Melbourne that I was giving up, as I couldn't take it anymore. I thought that the Peaceful Bay Sleep Station was still far away. But to be honest, I was just a few metres away. Finally, I reached Peaceful Bay and I was only 5-10 minutes late. I saw the volunteers closing the station, as I was the last runner to check in. I also saw a few other runners, who checked in ten minutes before me and were resting there. One of the volunteers called the organisers to confirm whether I was DNF or if I could continue. The answer was negative. It was just a lesson for me that if I had not wasted those 15 minutes in the beach, I could have continued my journey. But to be honest, these were all lessons I learned. I reached the 204km mark and still had 146km to go, which is massive. The volunteer who drove back to me to the Denmark Sleep Station consoled me by saying that 204km is still a massive achievement and that I should be proud of that.

I immediately called my friends in Melbourne, who were tracking me through the race map, and told them the story of my failure. They were disappointed and yelled at me, telling me I wasted a lot of money in this event by quitting. I got their point; they badly wanted me to succeed, but the true journey of success is through failure. I wish I could have told them that. I am still grateful for when they yelled at me, as I realised that they really cared for me. I got a similar feeling when my relationship broke up with my family during my trip to India. My family yelled at me because they wanted me to succeed, but we all need to fail in life multiple times in order to get a glimpse of success. I wish I could send this message to every parent in India and around the world: failing is a compulsory part of life. Please do not humiliate your children for failing in exams or in life. We all need to learn that every failure is a learning experience. Running 204km in 52 hours on 2.5 hours of sleep might not be a complete failure. I did what millions of people might not be able to achieve.

Such adventures teach me great life lessons.

## 8 lessons from the Delirious West 200 Miler:

### *1. Failing is Not a Crime, Lack of Effort is*

The Delirious West 200 Miler challenge is the story of my failure. I had almost given on the idea of writing a book on this adventure, but my good friend, Dr. Priya Virmani, called me from Kolkata, India, and encouraged me to continue with this project. The most important lesson I learnt is that failure is just a bend in the road, not end of the road.

We should never be scared to fail and learn new things. Every single person in this planet has failed at some point in their lives and this is one of the most important lessons I've learnt. We need to celebrate our failures. Our families, friends and loved ones need to support us and celebrate our failures. We have to fail 100 times in order to succeed once. The important thing is to not give up on our dreams and to keep trying. Remember, Thomas Edison failed several times before he invented the light bulb.

*'I have not failed. I have just found 10,000 ways that won't work'*

*'Our greatest weakness lies in giving up. The most certain way to succeed is always to try just one more time.'*
– Thomas Edison

Sometimes, after several rejections and failures, we give up on our dreams. This is natural, but at the same time, we need a good mentor to help us move forward. When I am thinking of giving up on a run, I always meet someone who motivates me and makes me realise why I do this and why it is important to me. I was very grateful I got the opportunity to take part in this adventure; it was a community-building event and one could have learnt so much just by looking at the spirit of these 64 incredible athletes. If it was easy, everyone would do it, so the 350km was tough and challenging. You need courage to reach the finish line of this event.

Every single person I met at this event, including runners, volunteers, organisers, support crew and pacers, had a story. They were chasing genius. They were trying to achieve something that very few in this world of 7 billion people can do. We live in a world where we often come across so much negative news. So, our minds become pessimistic as well. But when we do these kinds of challenges, we become positive and hopeful that the world is a beautiful place, despite the bad things happening around us.

To be honest, I became negative, so running ultramarathons helped me appreciate this beautiful life, practice gratitude and, most importantly, learn how to fail. I was disqualified from this challenge at around the 204km mark, but most importantly, I tried an extreme adventure that most people in this world wouldn't even think of doing. I remember meeting one runner named James, who told me how some of his friends got offended when he told them that he was trying to run 100 or 200 miles. Yes, in society, ultra-running is considered a niche sport. It is not an Olympic sport, but it's important that we run such long distances because it makes us feel good. It also makes us resilient and helps us build our confidence, appreciate the beauty of nature, eradicate mental illness and get a good night sleep when we are really tired. Do you know that millions of people in this world are not getting a good night sleep because of stress, anxiety and depression? Sleep deprivation takes a toll on our mental health, and I was surprised to read a report by the American Academy of Sleep Medicine that 70 million Americans have trouble getting a good night sleep. Another study says that sleep deprivation is a major problem in India and Australia as well. When I am running such long distances, I forget all my problems and get a good night sleep after events. I was hardly able to sleep well in this challenge, and I lost nearly 4kg, but I recovered well.

Most importantly, challenges not only teach us to fail but also how to survive in extreme situations involving snakes and bushfires. When I met James during the event, he taught me how to poop in a jungle. I was worried about this and carried toilet paper in case of an emergency call of nature. Luckily, I got to use the toilet at the Walpole Sleep Station and other sleep stations.

I felt like I went to school to learn and meet extraordinary people on this planet and came back home a better version of myself. Maybe someday I will do this challenge again – not to prove anything to anybody, but to follow my passion for running and my love for nature.

## 2. Ultra-Runners Love Nature

Yes, we love nature. Nature teaches us incredible lessons. As the saying goes, if we destroy nature, nature will destroy us. Many of the natural disasters in the world are man-made. We are greedy, wanting to make lots and lots of money, and we take nature for granted. As a result, climate change has become real. During the Covid-19 lockdown, we saw a tremendous drop in air pollution around the world. A picture of the Himalayas, now clearly visible from a North Indian state, went viral.

So, as a runner, I have learnt to respect nature and soak in its immense beauty. I am the happiest person in the world when I run in nature. I feel like I am talking to the trees, mountains and rivers, and they help me live a meaningful life. Nature is like a temple to me. I would prefer to spend my time in nature than in an air-conditioned room. I recharge myself by running in nature. It is my fuel. It teaches me how to love humanity and feel every cell of my body.

Often, we live in a world surrounded by tech giants and apps, and we are glued to our phones, looking for happiness. There is no doubt that technology is essential to our lives, but we cannot be completely dependent on it for our happiness. Sometimes, cooking and baking gives us happiness. Sometimes, going for a hike in the mountains gives us happiness. Sometimes, having great relationships gives us happiness. So, my point is, our secret to happiness might vary, but we live in a world where nature is an essential part of our lives. We need to appreciate its beauty and be grateful that we are living in places surrounded by flora and fauna. Loving nature or spending time in nature is like spending time with your pet; it gives you a meaning in life and a connection.

It is said that gardening is a stress-buster, just like baking. Nature could be used as medicine for stress and anxiety. It has the ability to make us feel better. Often, we take everything that nature offers us for granted, like water, fresh air and food. But as a runner, I have learned to practice gratitude when I am in nature. I know that millions of people who live in extreme poverty in India and Africa cannot afford to enjoy the beauty of nature, I saw in the Delirious West event.

We need to save our planet and take care of it. Imagine a world where people are giving up their cars at least once a week to start running, walking and cycling. The world would be better off. Our planet depends on the mindset of 7 billion people. If I can educate some people about the importance of a healthy environment, climate change and why loving nature is important, I might be able to make this world a better place.

## 3. *Sometimes in Life There Are No Limits*

Have you seen the movie *Limitless*? Hollywood actor Bradley Cooper takes a pill and becomes 'limitless.' He develops the power to read minds and learn various languages, and he makes a fortune by using these abilities to solve any problem. This is not possible in real life. There are limits and hurdles that we need to learn to conquer. By doing this 350km challenge, I was trying to get out of my comfort zone. Our lives are never going to be easy and I was trying to learn how to live with purpose, passion, compassion and kindness by having an adventure.

### 4. *Mental Fitness is More Important Than Physical Fitness*

I have seen people living in mansions who feel lonely. I have seen people with six-pack abs who have suicidal thoughts. I have seen people become rich and famous, only to find out that these things are not the answer, and commit suicide. We live in a world where society will call you successful if you become rich and famous, but if that is the definition of success, why do movie stars also end their lives? So, my point is that mental health is a very big issue in the world right now, especially during this pandemic, and a lot of people have given up on life because they have no hope.

Mental fitness is more important than physical fitness. I am not saying that physical fitness is not important, but running long distances is an example of mental fitness; one has to push their limits to reach the finish line. The race is so long that there will be times when we will be completely drained of energy, but in those moments we need to explore our mental strength. Ultra-running is a sport that has taught me how to be both physically and mentally fit. One of my favourite sports stars in the world is former Indian cricketer Sachin Tendulkar, who says that in order to excel in any sport, we need to be physically, as well as mentally, fit.

'We need to be at peace with ourselves and learn how to handle external pressure by dealing with our own mind', says Sachin. I always try to think of him when I am running ultramarathons. The world can learn so much from the way Tendulkar handles pressure and failure.

## 5. *Finding Our Purpose is Important in Life*

When I wrote my first book, *Limitless Humans*, many people told me I had found my purpose. I wish to run marathons and write books in my life. Maybe someday I will also make short movies. My purpose is to create an impact in this world, whether it be through books, movies, podcasts, speaking engagements, improv comedy, art or cooking.

I do so many things in my life that even my family aren't sure about who I truly want to become. I guess this is a problem that many people in this world who struggle to find their purpose and meaning in life face. I am in my element when I am running marathons, just like how an actor feels confident acting in a movie.

If we all find our purpose in life, the world will be a better place and we will all live life to the fullest. Most people in this world don't know where they are going; they are blindly chasing the two metrics of success – money and power – in this so-called rat-race. If all of us find our purpose, there will be more people like Steve Jobs, Mark Zuckerberg, Jeff Bezos and Sundar Pichai.

Unfortunately, it is said that we are born creative geniuses, but the education system dumbs us down. The education system prepares us for this race without telling us that life is not a race, but more like an ultramarathon, with ups and downs and different timelines. There are people who change careers at age 50 because they are living someone else's life and are not truly happy.

There are people who get married at 35 and find the right partner to be really happy with. Often, our society and families put pressure on us, but there is no book in the world that says we all have to find our purpose by a certain age. Steve Jobs found his purpose at age 21, and I found my purpose at age 30. The most important thing is to love what we do and get up each day with a purpose in life. That is how to create an impact in someone else's life.

## 6. 'Our Prime Purpose in Life is to Help Others, and if You Can't Help Them, at Least Don't Hurt Them' – The Dalai Lama

I have been following the Dalai Lama for a while now, and I believe his teachings are still relevant today. We need world peace. We need love, kindness and compassion. We need to treat people with respect. One thing running has taught me is to have the courage to follow my heart and create an impact in someone else's life.

When I wrote my first book, *Limitless Humans*, I got this text message from someone who has been struggling with jail time and drugs:

'G'day mate. I'm up to page 57 and love your book. It feels like it was actually written for me. I've spent a lot of time in and out of jail; I was an obese drug addict/alcoholic and I've spent time in psych wards. Anxiety was a major contributor to my drinking, but now I've been sober since New Year's Day 2019 and haven't used ice since September 2018. I agree with you – running can change your life. Tomorrow, I'm riding my mountain bike up the Geelong rail trail in a 100km virtual challenge, then next month, on the 8th of June, I'm doing my first marathon on my 44th birthday as a way to celebrate my new life sober instead of getting drunk. I felt like sharing this with you because, like I said, your book feels like it was written for me. I say G'day to every person I encounter and every day on Facebook. I post good morning messages to hopefully put a SMILE on the faces of my friends who still struggle with drugs and jail, and to give them hope. I also think I told you I'm planning on doing the surf coast century this year.'

The above text message just made my day. I was able to create an impact in someone else life by writing a book. So, the biggest lesson here is to have the attitude to help others, to chase humanity. There should be no place for jealousy, hatred or comparison in our lives. Someone will always be better than me in some way. Our purpose is to become the best versions of ourselves. While I was reading Oprah Winfrey's book, *What I Know for Sure*, I came across a line that struck me like a bolt:

'The truth is that nay-sayers in your life can never be fully satisfied. Whether you hide or shine, they will always feel threatened because they don't believe they are enough. Stop paying attention to them. Every time you suppress some part of yourself or allow others to play you small, you are ignoring the owner's manual your creator gave you.'

I connected so well with this and realised that I couldn't make every individual happy in this world. There will be always someone who will hate you. Being positive in this negative world is not a sign of weakness, but a sign of strength. When I am running an ultramarathon, I am giving hope to millions of people that if I can do it, so can they. At the end of the day, before we die, our purpose should be found.

## 7. *Sometimes You Will Make More Human Connections in a Jungle, Where There is No Wi-Fi*

This was one of the most important lessons I learned from the Delirious West 200 Miler. I met some extraordinary people and built friendships that might last forever. Often, we live in big cities surrounded by technology.

When I moved to Melbourne, I realised that everyone was running after one thing: money in a neo-liberalism model. The whole structure was designed in such a manner where, without money, you couldn't survive. It became our primary goal and we sacrificed our health and relationships to get a certain bank balance.

Once we get the fortune we were chasing, we realise that our health and relationships were suffering, which contributes to mental illness. When we spend time in nature, or go on an adventure, we are at least making connections with nature and humans. For me, making human connections in this digital world is very important.

## 8. 'A Man who Risks Nothing Gains Nothing' – Bear Grylls

I grew up watching Bear Grylls' show *Man vs. Wild*. In it, he says that a man who risks nothing gains nothing. I have read most of his books, and his journey always inspired me to take part in adventures. But at the same time, we need to take calculated risks. I made sure I carried all the correct gear, and trust me, running whole nights like a crazy person can kill you. I took risks, but calculated risks. In life, we need to make key decisions and risks at the right times.

I took the risk of doing this challenge as I felt there was a possibility of watching the stars at night and the world with wonder. I remember the skin under my feet on my left leg coming off. I saw the swollen leg of a runner. We will never forget this experience of a lifetime. Maybe we will take it with us forever. The lesson here is that we need to take calculated risks in life sometimes. Steve Jobs, and some of the other most successful entrepreneurs in this world, take risks. They are not afraid to fail.

> I remember Steve Jobs saying in one of his speeches, 'When I was 17, I read a quote that went something like: "If you live each day as it was your last, someday you'll most certainly be right." It made an impression on me, and since then, for the past 33 years, I have looked in the mirror every morning and asked myself: "If today were the last day of my life, would I want to do what I am about to do today?" And whenever the answer has been "No" for too many days in a row, I know I need to change something. Remembering that I'll be dead soon is the most important tool I've ever encountered to help me make big choices in life. Almost everything – all external expectations, all pride, all fear of embarrassment or failure – these just fall away

in the face of death, leaving only what is truly important. Remembering that you are going to die is the best way I know to avoid the trap of thinking you have something to lose. You are already naked. There is no reason not to follow your heart.'

This is so true. I believe we all want to go to heaven, but none of us want to die. There is nothing to lose. I was not scared to die and take calculated risks in the Delirious West challenge.

We have got to risk everything. 'The greatest artists like Dylan. Picasso and Newton risked failure. If we want to be great, we've got to risk it too,' Jobs added. Another great entrepreneur, Mark Zuckerberg, said 'purpose is what creates true happiness. The greatest successes come from having the freedom to fail.'

If you want to know what my purpose is, it is to run marathons and to inspire people by telling them that I am not afraid to fail.

| Aid Station Name | Distance from previous Aid | Accum distance | Distance from finish |
|---|---|---|---|
| Northcliffe Start Line | 0 | 0 | 350.7 |
| Chesapeake Rd (West) | 23.9 | 23.9 | 326.8 |
| Chesapeake Rd (East) | 17.6 | 41.5 | 309.2 |
| Dog Rd | 11.7 | 53.2 | 297.5 |
| Pingerup Rd | 18 | 71.2 | 279.5 |
| Brooke Inlet Rd | 16.3 | 87.5 | 263.2 |
| Mandalay Beach Rd | 21.8 | 109.3 | 241.4 |
| Deep River Crossing | 19.6 | 128.9 | 221.8 |
| Walpole (SLEEP STATION) | 11.9 | 140.8 | 209.9 |
| Giant Tingle Tree | 9.8 | 150.6 | 200.1 |
| Tree Top Walk | 22.4 | 173 | 177.7 |
| Conspicuous Beach | 15.8 | 188.8 | 161.9 |
| Peaceful Bay (SLEEP STATION) | 15.2 | 204 | 146.7 |
| Boat Harbour Rd | 23.4 | 227.4 | 123.3 |
| Parry Beach | 10.6 | 238 | 112.7 |
| William Bay | 7.6 | 145.6 | 105.1 |
| Monkey Rocks | 9.9 | 255.5 | 95.2 |
| Denmark River Mouth (SLEEP STATION) | 11.9 | 267.4 | 83.3 |
| Eden Rd | 10 | 277.4 | 73.3 |
| Lowlands Beach | 14.7 | 292.1 | 58.6 |
| Shelley Beach | 17.1 | 309.2 | 41.5 |
| Cosy Corner (SLEEP STATION) | 7.8 | 317 | 33.7 |
| Mutton Bird Carpark | 9.3 | 326.3 | 24.4 |
| Sandpatch Carpark | 13.2 | 339.5 | 11.2 |
| South Coast Progress Assoc Hall (FINISH) | 11.2 | 350.7 | 0 |

*This was my bible and I was carrying it in my backpack.*
*Name of every aid and sleep stations.*

*My running profile*

*With Breeze Sharma and Glenn Monaghan at Northcliffe*

*Some of the track*

*With other participants*

# Chasing Humanity

I live in a world where all of my friends are busy chasing so called 'success'; money, power, job status, citizenship, a big house, a big car …. There is nothing wrong with this, but I will ask one thing: are we missing humanity in the world right now? When I run marathons, I try to redefine what success is. I am chasing humanity. I wish to build life and inspire people who have given up on life. In this current era of Covid-19, the world is not going to be the same again. Stress levels are at all-time highs, as millions of people have lost their jobs.

An estimated 350 million people around the world suffer from depression, which affects the economy deeply. In the US, suicide rates are at a thirty-year high. In Australia, 1-3 people commit suicide every day and many of these cases don't even get reported. Due to the Covid-19 crisis, there was massive panic-buying in Australia and other first world countries. Can you imagine how much food and toilet paper was wasted in this panic buying? Every day, we throw away more food in our homes, restaurants and supermarkets than it would take to feed one billion people who live in extreme poverty and can't even afford basic necessities like food, clothing and shelter. When Australians were fighting for toilet paper in March

2020, I wished they were fighting for books. If they had, the world could have been a better place today.

We should be chasing humanity instead of fighting for toilet paper and material things that have no value. In every marathon I ran, I tried to inspire people and help them create meaningful changes in their lives. I spoke with people who came from a dazzling array of socioeconomic, ethnic and cultural backgrounds, and people who suffered from mental illnesses. I have been a follower of the Dalai Lama for a while now and he defines compassion as:

> 'A state of mind that is non-violent, non-harming and non-aggressive. It is a mental attitude based on the wish for others to be free of their suffering and is associated with a sense of commitment, responsibility and respect towards others.'

If we become compassionate towards one another and treat people with respect, then I assume half of the world's problems would be solved.

My friends who aren't chasing genius want money and power. This is great, there is nothing wrong with that, but I will ask two things: what are you doing to make this world a better place, and what are you doing for the millions of people in this world who live in extreme poverty and suffer from mental illness? If you ask me what I am doing, I would say that I am running marathons for myself and writing this book for every soul who has given up on life.

There is a saying that 'everybody wants to go to heaven but nobody wants to die.' Similarly, everybody wants to be rich and wealthy and nobody wants to be poor. Poverty is not a great thing, yet the destination of success or becoming wealthy is through hard work, struggle and maybe even living in extreme poverty.

## Is Driving a Luxurious Car Considered Success, or is Running 100km and 200km Ultramarathons Considered Success?

All of us want to achieve so-called 'success,' but the road to success is paved with a lot of pain and hardship, which we often forget. I often ask my friends, who love boasting about their new luxurious cars on social media, if they call this success or temporary happiness. Permanent happiness comes from helping others and giving hope to millions of people, who have given up on life. When I run 100km or 200km ultramarathons, I give hope to millions of people who can't imagine running even 200m. I give hope to disabled people who are considered insubstantial and who are not treated like they are important in the world. I give hope to Aboriginal people and people of colour who face various challenges and racism while trying to live meaningful lives. There are many barriers in front of people within the LGBTQI+ community, who also face discrimination from society. So, my point is, when I run long distance, I empower every single soul in this planet who deals with their own challenges and societal stress.

As Eulid Kipchoge said, 'no human is limited.' We all have the potential to become the best version of ourselves by running marathons or by doing something meaningful in our lives. There is nothing wrong with driving expensive cars or boasting on social media, but I will always ask whether you also have the ability to inspire people by doing something extraordinary. It could be anything from climbing mountains, running ultramarathons or dancing on a popular TV show like *America's Got Talent.*

I often think of American poet, Maya Angelou, who said, 'if you are always trying to be normal, you will never know how amazing you can be.'

We all have the strength inside us to achieve greatness, but sometimes there is so much noise telling us that we are not good enough. By chasing greatness, I do not only mean realising your full potential, but also realising your full potential to make an impact in the lives of others. Every one of us has the ability to inspire another soul. I love this next quote from Maya Angelou, 'You can only become truly accomplished at something you love.'

For me, running marathons in nature is what I love the most. I am in my element when I run marathons and ultramarathons. I've realised that I have the ability to inspire many individuals who have given up on life. I always try to achieve greatness in my running. When people watch me following my dreams, they love it as well. So, I can only become truly accomplished by running marathons or writing a book – by doing something I love. I enjoy writing and don't do it for fame and money.

Imagine if we all started doing something meaningful in our lives – it would save our humanity and make life better for others. You could create a product for people to use. You could influence and inspire them. Imagine the world without Google, Facebook, Apple and Amazon. These tech giants not only changed the world, but also left their mark on Earth. As long as people are alive, they will use either Google, YouTube or Gmail. The world is more connected today with Facebook, WhatsApp and other social media platforms.

We all have the ability to create something that could change the lives of others. It could be running ultramarathons, writing a book, cooking, dancing and even making movies. The only thing is, we have to be best at it, as there will always be competition. While I am writing this book, someone at the same time is writing a better book than me. While I am running 100km and 200km ultra marathons and boasting on social media, someone is running a 350km or 500km ultramarathon without posting anything on social media. There will always be extraordinary humans around us who chase humanity and make this world a better place. We need to learn from their greatness.

**What is the Purpose Of My Life?**

I often ask myself, what is the purpose of my life? I realised my purpose when I just turned 30 last year. I wish to run marathons across the world, write books and even make videos and movies. I believe books and movies have the ability to shift culture and create a huge impact in the lives of others. There are so many global problems in the world right now, such as Covid-19, climate change, poverty, racism and mental illness. All of these problems have been created by humans, and all humans have the ability to solve them. I wish to make this world a better place by running marathons. When I run marathons, nobody questions the colour of my skin or my background. I feel I can integrate myself in the world by doing something I love the most. I live in the present and forget all my problem when I run.

I remember what the Dalai Lama once said about humanity:

> 'Man! Because he sacrifices his health to make money. Then he sacrifices his money to recuperate his health. And then he is so anxious about the future that he does not enjoy the present; the result being that he does not live in the present or future; he lives as he is never going to die, and then dies having never really lived.'

I connected so deeply to this phrase when I am running, I forget all my problems and live in the present. What if I die tomorrow? Why are we so scared about the future that we don't enjoy the present? We live in a world today where uncertainty and levels of anxiety are at all-time highs. There are some things that are beyond our control, but what is in our control is mindfulness. We need more people in the world who can teach us the art of living, because so many people have forgotten how to live a meaningful life. We can only live a purposeful life by doing the things we love most. I understand that the majority of people in this world who live in extreme poverty have no dreams to follow except for their immediate priority to uplift themselves from impoverishment. People who come from extremely poor backgrounds have to struggle more and there are many hurdles towards their success and dreams. We live in a world today where the rich are getting richer and poor are getting poorer. But with hard work and determination, anything is possible. However, people who come from middle or upper-middle classes can definitely find their purpose, and can choose to use their skills to make a living or to just pursue their hobbies.

I am not the best ultramarathon runner in the world, and I am also not the best author, but I am willing to sacrifice and undergo training to reach perfection. I believe that if I can inspire one individual through my book, runs or YouTube Videos, my life is worth living. Trust me – many people don't know their purpose of life. They are blindly chasing success in a rat-race. How often do you see people with careers such as a poet, a philosopher, a motivational speaker, a YouTuber or even a marathon runner? There is so much noise out there from society, parents, workplaces and school that many people give up on their dreams. But I would say it is completely ok to live any life. For many, driving 100km is considered success. For a few, running 100km is considered success. We can't change social perceptions. We are just here to follow our dreams and make life purposeful and meaningful for ourselves and other members of the human race.

## Tell Your Haters to Back Off, Because You are Chasing Humanity

Here is one thing I have always observed: whenever someone is trying do something extraordinary in this world, there will be someone who will criticise or hate them. I will just say this to such people: haters, please back off. Ignore the nay-sayers. Elon Musk is such a great visionary who creates extraordinary things like rockets and electric cars for people to use. Such people inspire other humans to do something meaningful in their lives. Imagine if Elon Musk or Steve Jobs would have settled for ordinary jobs – the world would be so different today. I always tell my haters, the more you criticise me, the more I will run and chase humanity. My mission is to inspire people suffering from mental illness and I won't stop running anytime soon. People often hate you because they feel insecure. They consider you as a competition, but to be honest, there is no place for hatred or jealousy in my life. Life is too short for that. We are all programmed for generosity.

Since I was in school, I was told by my parents, teachers and friends that the secret to success is getting a dream job, a big house, a big car, a beautiful partner and, most importantly, wealth, power and a job title that we are proud of. Everybody told me to build my CV, but nobody told me to build a life or chase humanity. Our value is not determined by the price of our clothes or our job titles. Millions of people in this world need our help; they live in very difficult circumstances. My life, and the lives of my friends, are much better than theirs.

Yet, there is no doubt that money is important in life as well. It gives us a better life, and we can only help others if we help ourselves first. When I run marathons, or in my words, chase humanity, I am gaining inner peace. There are many people in this world, and even though they have wealth and power, they are still not happy. For some, happiness depends on having a certain job, possessing a luxurious car, a beautiful partner and lots of wealth. But will these things guarantee permanent happiness? If we practise gratitude and be grateful for the things we have instead of complaining about all the things we don't have, our lives will be more beautiful. For me, running a marathon and even a 100km ultramarathon is not a big deal anymore. But if I make myself a condition that I will only be happy if I win a marathon in a record time of 2 hours 10 minutes and win the prize money of $20,000, then I will never be happy. Having a goal and a dream is a great thing, but in case we fail, we should also learn to celebrate our failure, because without failure, there is no success.

**How Can I Inspire and Motivate the World?**

There are people in this world who want to do extraordinary things to inspire the world. But some people give up after a few failures. However, the person who keeps failing and who learns from every failure is able to chase greatness. There is so much pain in the world we live in today, but such pain also makes us strong. Losing my mother in April 2002 was one of the most painful moments in my life, but it also opened other opportunities for me.

Many of us hope we will never have to encounter serious difficulties or challenges in our lives, but my own experiences have taught me that if I had not encountered great difficulties and suffering, I would have never had a chance to grow in my running journey. I would have never realised that I was born to run marathons. I learned how to heal, transform and touch profound peace, joy and freedom by running marathons. As someone has rightly said, 'no pain, no gain.' We all want a beautiful body with six-pack abs, but we forget how much discipline and hard work one has to undergo in order to achieve this. Running marathons also taught me to be compassionate and kind. It made me realise that happiness also comes from suffering and pain.

Many people know the success of British author J.K. Rowling, but very few know how much pain she went through in order to become the highest paid author in the world. We often forget about the pain and struggles faced by others when we see them succeed, but trust me, every one of us has gone through some kind of pain and struggle in our lives. Even if you were born with a silver spoon in your mouth, you still have to go through some kind of struggle – it's just that your struggle or pain might be bit lesser than others.

I was often compared to other students at school and university, and I was told I was not good enough. If I started caring about what others thought of me, I wouldn't have been able to live. To be honest, there is no rat-race and no Fitbit in the world that has the ability to monitor my strength. No device can tell me how much I can run and in what time. My ability is limitless and every time I run a distance; I try to get better at it. I remember failing physics, chemistry and maths in year 11. I was never meant to study science. I took art in year 12 and scored 80 percent. We are often compared to others in school, university or the workplace. Sometimes, we feel worse about ourselves when we see our friends doing well on social media, but we all have different timelines. Our ultimate aim in life should be to chase humanity or achieve personal greatness.

If I buy my house at age 35 or 40, it is still an achievement, as millions of people in this world are homeless. We often complain that our lives are not that great, that we are tired after doing same work again and again, but what about poor labourers in some of the difficult parts of the world, who work in extreme environments? They risk their lives and get paid less than we could ever imagine. In this world, you die the same day you are born, if you're part of a poor family. Poverty is not a great thing. It takes away your self-confidence. We all have the ability to inspire people to become the best version of themselves. Ortega launched Zara when he was 39. Jack Ma started Alibaba when he was 35. Morgan Freeman got his big break at around 50. Elon Musk launched Space X at 30. I have seen people running marathons at 18 and 101 years old. Yes, I am talking about British-Indian Marathon runner Fauja Singh, who has been deemed the oldest marathon runner in the world. So, everyone has different timelines.

I recognised the importance of running 10 years ago. Fauja Singh knew this when he was 80. It's never too late to follow a dream or a hobby and it's never too late to inspire people. But before we die, we should all leave our mark on the world.

If we can create meaningful, purposeful and fulfilling lives for ourselves and others by inspiring people to do something substantial in their lives, life is worth living. But the most important thing is to be truthful and meaningful in our lives. When I fail in my marathons, I post about my failure on social media. We need to accept failure as much as we love showing off strength and success. The truth is, we have all suffered from stress and anxiety in some part of our lives, so there is no shame in sharing those feelings. We love sharing our happy moments to show others how beautiful our lives are, but you should also share your suicidal thoughts after a breakup on social media. There will be one true friend out of the thousands of friends you have who will come forward and speak with you about your problems. We all feel lonely sometimes, as there is so much competition and pressure to succeed in life, but there is no rat-race. Every one of us has a different timeline and we all have the ability to chase humanity.

## Why Do I Love Nature So Much?

Chasing humanity is one of the most beautiful things in the world, and people who chase humanity also love being in nature. I love running in nature; in fact, every marathon runner or trail runner have I met lately has some kind of close association with nature. We love spending time in nature as it is so beautiful and it helps us realise our full potential.

Humans are seekers of knowledge and beauty. Nobody wants to live in a polluted environment, yet millions of poor people in this world have no other option. When I run marathons, I always search for ways to look at this world from a different point of view. I connect to my spiritual self and look for experiences that give me great joy and human connections. For me, running in nature and making human connections in this digital world are more important than spending all day in front of computer screen. Mindfulness is the need of the hour and we need to spend time in nature in order to realise our potential.

Yes, I do love running indoor on the treadmill – it gives me joy and energy. Running on the treadmill and running outdoors both give me joy, but nature teaches us some great lessons, such as how important it is to preserve it. We need to maintain a relationship with nature. If we destroy nature, nature will destroy us, and one of the biggest changes we face is climate change. Nature gives us life and hope. Without it, none of us would be able to thrive.

This poem, in American poet and storyteller Maya Angelou's autobiography *I Know Why the Caged Bird Sings*, had a deep impact in the world. Today, we need similar thinkers, poets and storytellers. We don't need more 'successful' people – we need leaders, thinkers and visionaries who can make this world a better place. In her book, Maya Angelou raises lot of issues like racism, gender, freedom and what a woman of colour is capable of achieving. I believe her poems are still so relevant, especially when we are still struggling to fight racism.

We all want freedom, and I get my freedom when I run in nature. I forget all of my problems and live in the present. I believe that meditating for five minutes in nature every day, or once a week, could have a profound impact in our lives. After a run, I try to meditate for five minutes in nature. This gives me clear vision and clarity. It also helps me realise my goals and know how to overcome barriers to achieve them. This connection with nature gives me immense peace and joy.

I believe that, by connecting to nature, some of the world's greatest leaders have realised their full potential and learned from their failures. Steve Jobs dove into a spiritual quest and discovered his higher self during a trip to the Himalayas after being fired from his own company. He was considered a failure, but then he came up with NeXT Company, which Apple bought. So, spending time in nature can actually help us have vision and clarity in life. Bill Gates spends two weeks in the forest each year to connect to his spiritual self.

Surrounding ourselves with books and mindful meditation before bed, with no screen time, could be a game changer. Just switching off our phones and electronic devices before going to bed, and maybe reading a book, could help us so much.

The Prime Minster of India, Narendra Modi, also went on a spiritual quest at the age of 17, when he had no clarity and vision in his life.

> 'I was undecided and unguided and unclear. I didn't know where I wanted to go, what I wanted to do and why I wanted to do it. But all I knew was that I wanted to do something. So, I surrendered myself to God and left for the Himalayas at the age of 17. I bid goodbye to my parents as my mother gave me a sweet dish before I left and put a tilak on my forehead to bless my journey.' Prime Minister Modi shared his story, and his quest for spirituality, through his social media.

Some great thinkers and leaders have spent time in nature to realise their full potential and find their purpose. Tech titans Steve Jobs (Apple) and Mark Zuckerberg (Facebook) went to Kainchi Dham Ashram in Northern India to mull the future of their companies, which changed the world. But this does not mean everyone in the world should go to the forest or become a monk to realise their full potential. We can realise our potential by sitting in a room, or by doing what we love. Yet, there is no doubt that spending time in nature helps. We can all become what we dream of by doing what we love and by inspiring others through our journeys.

## Does What We Eat Affect our Thinking and Human Behaviour?

My thinking towards human development also changed when I started consuming more green vegetables, like spinach, on a daily basis. I love chicken and fish, but I decided to take a break and eat a strictly green diet. Trust me, your entire thinking process changes when you consume healthy foods like green vegetables and fruits. One of the most important things to have is discipline in our eating habits. My only bad habit, which I am trying to get rid of, is drinking soft drinks like Coca Cola and Pepsi. I have never enjoyed drinking alcohol and I don't smoke. Our good eating habits lead us to spirituality and help us recover from mental illness. We can become more positive in life by eating a healthy meal each day. Millions of people who live in extreme poverty can't even afford to purchase the meals that I consume on a daily basis.

## How Much Does an Ultramarathoner Sleep and How Can Sleep Affect Human Behaviour?

If we want to chase humanity, help others and make a difference in the world, we need to take care of our health. Sleeping is one of the best ways to remain healthy. I often try to get a good night's sleep before a big run. Sleeping eight hours at night is highly recommended.

When I read a book about the importance of sleep by Arianna Huffington, called *The Sleep Revolution*, I took the importance of sleeping seriously. Often, the people around me love saying that they are working so hard that they don't have time to sleep, but the fact is, sleep increases our performance at work. It helps us build strong relationships and, as an athlete, it enhances my running performance. I also believe sleep deprivation is an epidemic; there is a deep correlation between sleep deprivation and mental illness.

According to Harvard Medical School, sleep deprivation can affect our mental health, and sleep problems are particularly common in people who have anxiety, depression, bipolar disorder and attention deficit hyperactivity disorder (ADHD). Often, people suffering from mental illnesses have experienced sleep disorders.

After I run ultramarathons, I get a great sleep because I am physically and mentally exhausted. There is no doubt that exercise helps us sleep better. Our minds and bodies are gifts – we need to take care of them. Often, we take care of our body but we forget to take care of our brain. When I am about to give up during a long run, I use my mind to push my limits. There is a mutual relationship between our minds and sleep.

When we have negative thoughts, we suffer from mental illness, and as a result we do not get a healthy sleep. So, making our minds positive, even when we are surrounded by negativity, is a challenge. Studies have suggested that a good night's sleep enhances our mental and emotional intelligence and leads us towards positive thinking. We are living in a world where negative thinking and emotional vulnerability are at all-time highs. There are a few ways that we can become more positive: by sleeping, running, eating healthier and having strong relationships and deep human connections.

I believe all of these options are equally important, and that getting an adequate amount of sleep can actually help us alleviate symptoms of mental health problems. Research from Harvard says that there are many factors that contribute to sleep disorders.

One of the most important things in life is our lifestyle. I am grateful I don't drink, smoke or take any forms of drugs. However, I love my coffee. Alcohol depresses the nervous system and helps some people fall asleep, but its effects do not last long, and as a result, people wake up again. Not sleeping next to our phones and electronic devices also help us sleep better. For me, physical activity is a must to get better sleep. Meditation, deep breathing exercises and yoga can help us sleep better.

Every time I run a marathon, I meditate and counter any negative thoughts. People often call me 'marathon man' and I feel good about it because I enjoy and live every moment when I run. It gives me confidence, and most importantly, I get a better sleep. According to *WHO*, depression will take over heart disease and any other disease in the next few years. The *WHO* data reveals that close to 800,000 people die from suicide every year, which is one person every 40 seconds. Just listening to this figure gives me goosebumps. These people are not dying by road accidents or by disease – they are killing themselves. If mental illness can be helped, I believe that more than half of the world's problems could be solved. The data also suggests that for each adult who dies by suicide, more than 20 people are attempting it.

I wish to teach these people, through my books, that running helps and can be something meaningful in life. Feeling good about ourselves is helpful. We also need strong relationships and deep human connections. If we can do this, then we might be able to get an eight hour sleep.

Researchers at Harvard have asserted that depressed patients who experience insomnia and other sleep disturbances are more likely to experience suicidal thoughts. When I was reading *The Sleep Revolution* by Arianna Huffington, I came across this line: 'getting the right amount of sleep enhances the quality of every minute we spend with our eyes open.' This applies to ultramarathoners. If athletes are running 100 or 200 miles, they might only sleep for four hours, or even less. Getting adequate sleep before a race, and sleep after a race for recovery, is essential.

Sleep deprivation among children is also a very big issue. Fast food consumption and sleeping disorders can make a child emotionally unstable, so I really recommend getting them into sports, which may help us solve the sleep crisis. Indeed, we are in a midst of a sleep crisis, and sleep deprivation leads to mental illness. We should not take our sleep for granted and we all can only make this world a better place by sleeping one night at a time. Achieving peak performance in a job interview, or in any sporting event for an athlete, is only possible by getting proper sleep. We also need to change our lifestyle. There are behavioural strategies we can learn so that we can sleep better, live a better life and chase humanity.

## Be Kind to One Another

I have always been a big fan of American comedian Ellen DeGeneres, who talks about the importance of being kind to one another. I love how, on her TV show, she rewards people who do remarkable acts of kindness in their day to day lives. After watching her shows and reading her book, I felt that the world needed to start a kindness campaign. Every time I run a marathon, I wish I can inspire people who can't even run 100m. I have often come across people motivating one another and showing random acts of kindness, like helping a person who is struggling to finish a race. Karma is real. People will treat us the same way we treat them.

In September 2019, the University of California was announced as the first institute in the world to study kindness. The university is conducting research on the importance of volunteering and kindness and how it affects our mental health. This is such a fascinating study, as the world needs some real acts of kindness. When there are problems such as inequality and racism, a small act of kindness can make this world a better place. Just imagine being able to programme the world to follow a simple act of kindness. World leaders and celebrities could start preaching about the importance of kindness and why helping a person in need is important.

One of the biggest lessons I've learned in my life is how being kind has helped me become a good runner and a good human being. We are all born to be generous, but we are educated for greed. The schools and university I attended never taught me about acts of kindness. I was just told that life is a race and you have to chase so-called 'success': money and power. Running marathons has taught me that I have to chase humanity as well.

Imagine if the study of kindness and mindfulness was made compulsory in every university and every school in the world. There would be fewer problems involving drugs and gun violence in schools in America. There would be no bullying in schools and students would realise that their true purpose in life is to give back to the world.

I often ask myself, why does a person give up their seat on a train or tram? What are the implications of people volunteering in events like ultramarathons? Volunteering is nothing but giving back, building community and giving hope and inspiration to many. In many countries, volunteering is compulsory, and social work and community service are assigned to people as a punishment.

# Life is Too Short, So Help Others

When I hear about people ending their own lives, I always wonder what was going wrong and why we are failing as a society. There is very little humanity left in this world, as everyone is busy chasing success. Our lives are so short and the Covid-19 pandemic has taught us so many lessons. We need to bring humanity back, and that is only possible by helping others – by helping people in need. One thing I can proudly say is that running marathons has taught me to practice gratitude and help people in need.

In order to help people in need, I need to achieve so-called 'success': money and power. But why don't I keep helping people on my way to success? What if I get success after 10 years by building my projects? What if a natural disaster strikes and we lose our lives? This pandemic has proved that the world won't be the same again and life is too short. We need to build lives, along with building our CVs. It's about finding this balance in your life.

## Ancient Buddhism

Because suicide rates across the world are rising during this pandemic, I feel that we are failing as a society. We need to go back to ancient wisdom and dig deep into books that teach us about how to live a meaningful life.

For me, the secret to success lies in relationships, but we are failing to make meaningful human connections in this digital world. Over 29 million WhatsApp messages are sent per minute, according to official WhatsApp statistics as of May 2018, but we still feel lonely in general. One in four CEOs suffer from depression. We need more human connections and stronger relationships. Our quality of life does not depend on our job status, money or power, but on our relationships.

I am a follower of Gautama Buddha and the Dalai Lama and I always ask myself what the purpose of my life is: is it to run marathons, write books, cook my favourite meals, paint or sketch, serve the community or chase humanity? The clear answer I get is: serve humanity by running marathons, the thing I love the most in life. As Gautama Buddha said: 'There is no path to happiness: Happiness is the path.'

When I am running a trail or a beautiful track, I am on a path to happiness. Our prime purpose in life is to be happy and ancient wisdom helps us live meaningfully by teaching us to do what we love and have great human connections.

Some of Gautama Buddha's quotes and quotes from other thinkers had a deep impact in my life. I started questioning my very existence after reading the following:

*'It is better to be hated for what you are, than to be loved for what you are not.'*

André Gide

*'In the end only three things matter: how much you loved, how gently you lived, and how gracefully you let go of things not meant for you.'*

*'Buddha was asked, "what have you gained from meditation?" He replied, "Nothing! However, let me tell you what I have lost; anger, anxiety, depression, insecurity, fear of old age and death."'*

Alvin Alexander

*'The root of suffering is attachment.'*

*'All that we are is the result of what we have thought.'*

*'What you think, you become. What you feel, you attract. What you imagine, you create.'*

*'Nothing can harm you as much as your own thoughts unguarded.'*

*'Do not dwell in the past, do not dream of the future, concentrate the mind on the present moment.'*

'No one saves us but ourselves. No one can and no one may. We ourselves must walk the path.'

'Don't rush anything, when the time is right, it will happen.'
Unknown

'Your work is to discover your world and then with all your heart give yourself to it.'

'The whole secret of existence is to have no fear.'
Swami Vivekananda

'You will not be punished for your anger, you will be punished by your anger.'

'Health is the greatest gift, contentment is the greatest wealth, a trusted friend is the best relative, liberated mind is the greatest bliss.'

'The thought manifests as the word; the word manifest as the deed; the deed develops into habit; and habit hardens into character; so watch the thought and its way with care, and let it spring from love born out of concern for all beings ... as the shadow follows the body, as we think, so we become.'

*'When we meet real tragedy in life, we can react in two ways – either by losing hope and falling into self-destructive habits, or by using the challenge to find our inner strength.'*
Dalai Lama XIV

*'On the long journey of human life, faith is the best of companions.'*

*'A man who conquers himself is greater than one who conquers a thousand men in a battle.'*

*'All human unhappiness comes from not facing reality squarely, exactly as it is.'*

*'Those who are free of resentful thoughts surely find peace.'*

*'When the student is ready, the teacher will appear.'*
Tao Te Ching

*'It is during our darkest moments that we focus to see the light.'*
Aristotle

*'Holding onto anger is like drinking poison and expecting the other person to die.'*

*'To understand everything is to forgive everything.'*
*'Be kind to all creatures, this is the true religion.'*

*'If your compassion does not include yourself, it is incomplete.'*
Jack Kornfield

*'He who does not understand your silence, will probably not understand your words.'*
Elbert Hubbard

*'Believe nothing, no matter where you read it or who has said it, not even if I have said it, unless if it agrees with your own reason and your own common sense.'*

*'Happiness does not depend on what you have or who you are, it solely relies on what you think.'*

*'If you want to fly, give up everything that weighs you down.'*
Toni Morrison

I started reading books on Buddhism and connected so deeply with them. All of the above quotes changed the way I thought. I realised that if I applied these Buddhist teachings to my runs, I could perform better. If I forgave every person on this planet, I would be a happier person. If I meditated for just five minutes a day, I could realise my true potential. Mindfulness is the need of the hour. We all want to fly, but we are not willing to give up what it takes to fly. There is no place for jealously, hatred, anger, stress or anxiety in this world. It is time to be grateful for things we have, and for to those we don't. For example, I have 100 things to be grateful for: I am grateful that I am living in a developed country like Australia, that I have a job, that I can run 100km and 200km ultramarathons, that I can cook and paint and that I have food on my table every day, when millions of people in this world are living in extreme poverty. I am grateful that I live in a wonderful house with two housemates. So, you see, we all have so many things to be grateful for. Our desire for wealth and greed is so high that we often forget to breathe.

Life is not a race; it is a journey, and so are our goals. For some, their goal is to become wealthy, for others, it is to serve humanity. As Gautama Buddha said, 'Being kind to one another is our true religion.' When I run ultramarathons, I ask myself, what am I scared of? What is my fear? I take this as a challenge and calculate the risk behind it. We all want to be successful, but success does not come without taking risks. Success is achieved by having the right attitude and chasing compassion for one another.

## My Path to Happiness is Through Humanity

Having compassion for everyone can lead us to humanity. Often, we show kindness and compassion only to those we need in our lives, but what if we had the same attitude towards everyone? We need to be more human towards people who are in desperate need, like people from Indigenous backgrounds, members of the LGBTQI+ community and people with disabilities. People suffer from mental illness because of bad health and bad relationships. The medicine for this involves following the path of spirituality, mindfulness and humanity. Whenever I feel like I need to connect to my spiritual self, I run a marathon. Whenever I feel lonely in this chaotic digital world, I try to spend time in nature. Taking care of my financial wellbeing is equally important. We need money to do great work in this world. The problem starts when we become dependent on money for our happiness.

**Shut Out What Everyone Else Thinks and Have the Courage to Follow your Heart. You are Born for Something Unique and that is Running.**
American motivational speaker and author Wayne Dyer said, 'Don't die with your music still in you.' I love this, as we all have some kind of music within us but we are just too scared to play it. There is a book in everyone, but we are often ask ourselves, who would publish my book?, Who would buy my book, as I don't have five million followers on Instagram? We are not defined by our job status or the number of followers we have – we just need to be ourselves. Our spark – the value inside us – will not fade if we wear clothes that are not branded, or if we don't wear an Apple Watch.

At the end of the day, we will only be defined if we are able to find our purpose in this Earth, and if we are able to do what we love. I self-published my first book, *Limitless Humans*, and also sold few copies. So, don't let any noise stop you from following your dreams. We have very limited time on this Earth, and if we worry about the future, we forget to live in the present. I wish to live my life the best way possible. One rule in life I always follow is to smile. Even when I feel like the world is falling apart, I never forget to smile at a stranger or even to people we take for granted, like baristas, checkout people at supermarkets and cleaners.

Oprah Winfrey said, 'I don't want to just be successful in this world, I want to fulfill the highest, truest expression of myself as a human being.'

She is an observer for life. She realised she was God's child and through hard work, she made everything possible. You already have a spiritual life. There is no one creative like you – you are unique and have a unique gift, which only you have. Nobody can bring the uniqueness and authenticity that only you can bring. Your gifts and offerings to our planet are unique. While I have the ability to run long distances, you have the ability to do something creative. It is just a matter of realisation.

What we are all waiting for is a fulfilled, meaningful, sustainably joyful life. Constant empathy, compassion, kindness, gratitude and spiritual practices lead us to this. Every day, I try to write 5-10 things I am grateful for, because they bring me joy and happiness.

Martin Luther King Jr, once said, 'Not everyone can be famous but everyone can be great because greatness is determined by service.' We all have the ability to become the best version of ourselves by serving humanity. We all need to become the best in what we do, and if we do great things for humanity, we will always be remembered. I am not saying I am the best runner or author in the world, But I am chasing greatness. I learn something new every day, which inspires me to achieve greatness. We all have the ability to leave our mark in this world and prove to ourselves that we can have a great life.

## What Gives You Happiness: Food, Sex, Running or Chasing Humanity?

Often, we miss the beauty in our lives because we end up chasing something that doesn't give us permanent happiness. If I go for a run, I feel good for a day – a week at maximum. If I eat the food of my choice, I often feel good for a day before wishing to look for something else. The same applies to sex; it cannot give us permanent happiness. So, I often question how to live a truly authentic life and how to be happy in this chaotic world. I can only be happy by following my dreams, having great relationships and great health, and of course, by chasing humanity. One of my favourite storytellers and motivational speakers is Prince Ea, who shares some facts about airplanes:

> 'I learnt a fact about airplanes the other day. I was talking to the pilot and he told me that many of his passengers think that planes are dangerous to fly. Then he said, "it is a lot more dangerous for the plane to stay on the ground. On the ground, the plane starts to malfunction and rust, wear much faster than it was in the air." Then I thought, it makes total sense because planes were built to live in the sky, and every person was born to live their dreams that were built inside. So, the sad thing is to not live a life you were meant to without taking off,'

I resonate with this line, as we all have a gift inside of us; it is just a matter of realising it. If I just sit at home and eat without running for a long time, running even 200m would be a disaster. My body would rust like an aeroplane.

In 2019, I realised that I have a gift: I can run long distances and inspire people. We all have a gift inside us. You might be the best dancer in the world, or maybe there is a hidden art inside you, and you've never tried to find it because you were told that you were not good enough. Remember, Oprah Winfrey was told she was not fit for television and she became one of the most influential women on the planet. JK Rowling was rejected by 12 publishers and Steven Spielberg was rejected from film school. You see, our time is very limited and we have to follow our dreams and do something meaningful that also serves humanity.

Let me tell you another story. Johanna Quas, 94, is the oldest female gymnast in the world. While she was following her dreams of becoming a gymnast in her young age, she came across several barriers and had to make the difficult decision of giving up her dream to take care of her family and become a mother. But the most important lesson here is that it is never too old to chase your dreams. Morgan Freeman got his first big break in Hollywood at age 52. We are told by our families, teachers and friends that we are either too old or too young to follow our dreams. Truth to be told, it is never late to follow passion. When I run marathons, I see people aged 18-90 running with me. Marathon is a sport and there is no age limit for it. I feel that you always get better with age, as far as marathons are concerned. I can proudly say that running marathons has taught me another important lesson, and that is to never give up on your dreams, no matter how difficult the path is.

Let me tell you another story of a great athlete, wrestler and actor: Dwayne 'The Rock' Johnson. He went from having only seven bucks in his pocket to being one of the highest paid actors, and did this by remembering the hard times in his life. He was homeless when he was 14 and was arrested multiple times when he was 16 years old.

> 'Keep the hard times in front of the mind – that allows you to go into big moments. I have worked my ass off and you guys have worked your ass off. We can all have these big dreams but what is the anchor? The anchor is getting up at 4 o'clock in the morning before everybody else and grounding my thought process that no one will outwork me. I want to accomplish the world. I want Will Smith's career; I want to do it bigger and better. Remember where you came from? Keep that shit in front of your mind and when the shit goes back,' The Rock said in one of his most motivational and inspiring speeches of 2019.

He asserted that one needs to have a vision and stay focused, no matter what comes their way. So, the biggest lesson for us here is that we are all bound by humanity and have the power within us to do something great before we leave this world.

Truth to be told, I never had a clear vision in my life. I was always lost and was searching for something. My father was always worried about me. I felt like a medical student who studies to become a doctor; there's a 95 percent chance of ending up in a medical profession, unless you drop out to become an actor. But when you study an arts degree, your options are unlimited, and this creates confusion. I wanted to be a journalist. Now, I am an ultramarathon runner and an author. Tomorrow, I might become a stand-up comedian. I enjoy everything I do, but I also know that I am here to chase humanity and inspire millions of people who have given up on life with my work. We all have dreams, but very few of us have the courage to follow them. Dreams rely on hard work and a little bit of luck. I know that I will be running marathons for as long as I live. It makes me a confident person and it makes me feel good about myself.

It is just like when you hit the gym and pump up your muscles; it boosts your confidence. When I help an individual, it also boosts my confidence! My dad used to say that he felt confident because he helped his family with their financial needs. He used to do that because he was capable of it. So, becoming financially strong is also one of my goals, because without money, I can't chase humanity. People who blindly chase money and think that their ultimate goal is to become a millionaire or billionaire will not find ultimate happiness. Happiness is within us – we are born with it. Food and sex can give us temporary happiness but chasing humanity gives us permanent joy. I am able to connect with my spiritual self when I chase humanity and use my education to make a difference in the lives of others and the world.

# Power of Never Giving Up

## Stories of Powerful Human Beings Who Never Give Up, Even in Difficult Circumstances

No human is limited – that is, every human in this world has the potential to chase genius and never give up in difficult circumstances. Often, when I run marathons, I come across some extraordinary people who are chasing genius. I try to read their books and find out their stories; why are they so much more extraordinary than the rest of us? What are they chasing that some 'normal' humans are missing? We all are born with a gift, and that is storytelling. One extraordinary person is Bear Grylls, a British adventurer and host of one of the most watched shows on the planet, *Man vs. Wild*. Grylls inspires and teaches the world how to live a meaningful life by going on extreme adventures in some of the most difficult places on the planet. I grew up watching Grylls and have read almost all of his books. He teaches us how we can become mentally tough and resilient in extreme circumstances and to never give up. Life is sometimes as hard as a jungle to navigate, but when we face our fears, they often subside. As Grylls said, 'It is nearly impossible to get where you want to go, if you don't know where you want to go.'

In one of his motivational speeches, Grylls also said:

> 'My failures have forced me to adapt and stay resilient because there is no shortcut to any of our goals. You got to go through it if you want to succeed. Don't run from the failure. Failure is an essential marking and we need to pass through it. Life is scary sometimes and we often face battles. But whoever you are, life is going to test us all.'

I believe Grylls has a gift, but he was not born a superhuman who jumps from helicopters every day, which is what he does for a living. How many of us have the courage to do that? He is probably one of the most courageous men on the planet, and we can learn a lot from him.

One superhuman who inspires me is supermodel Gisele Bundchen. I was so inspired by her journey of fitness that I decided to read her book, *Lessons: My Path to a Meaningful Life*, several times before I wrote my first book, *Limitless Humans*. I connected so deeply to it because Bundchen so honestly shared her journey about how she lived in a small town in Brazil before becoming one of the world's top models, and about how she recovered from panic attacks by practicing yoga, eating healthy and taking care of her relationships. Her love for nature and her preaching for having a great life by having great relationships made me feel so connected to her wisdom. She is such a beautiful soul on this planet and inspires us to live meaningful lives by taking care of our physical and mental health. I advocate for the same things, but in the form of running marathons. It is my fuel and medicine for stress and anxiety.

Another limitless human on this planet is none other than Arnold Schwarzenegger, who broke the internet with his inspiring speeches. It's worth looking them up on YouTube. I was so inspired by his memoir, *Total Recall*. In his book, Schwarzenegger describes his journey from living in a small town in Austria to becoming a body building champion, playing the lead roles in Hollywood movies and becoming the Governor of California. America is a country of immigrants and Schwarzenegger describes how the country embraced his talent in order for him to achieve greatness:

> 'The first rule of success is to have a vision, and if you don't have a vision of where you are going, you will drift around and never end up anywhere. It's like, you can have the best ship in the world, the best airplane in the world, but if the pilot or captain doesn't know where to go, it would just drift around and will end up mostly in a wrong place. When you have a goal and a vision, everything becomes easy. [At] the age of 20, I went to London and won the Mr. Universe contest as the youngest Mr. Universe ever and it was because I had a goal. So, going after your goal and visualising it makes it fun. You got to have purpose, no matter what you do in life. The second rule is to ignore the naysayers. The third rule is to work like hell and then advertise. The fourth rule is to hate plan B and never be afraid to fail.'

These rules, written by Schwarzenegger about our journey to success, inspire us to stay irrepressible and never give up.

We have all failed at some point in our lives and there is no shame in that. The important lesson I learnt from Schwarzenegger's journey is that we all have to fail in order to succeed.

The world is better off with these motivational people. Every author in this world thinks of J.K. Rowling before writing their book. Yes, Rowling is another limitless human in the western world who, despite her challenges, became the highest paid author on the planet. We often receive rejections from publishers, which is very common in the book industry unless you have a large social media following. Let me tell you the story of J. K. Rowling, which inspired so many writers in the world to never give up, despite receiving rejections. In order to find out the secret to Rowling's success, I bought the first Harry Potter book.

There's a quotation in the first book that stuck with me: 'in magic, man has to rely on himself.'

In a powerful speech at the Harvard Commencement, Rowling said:

> 'But that's the perennial appeal of magic, the idea that we ourselves have power and we can shape our world. I came from a place where I was a single mother and it was really hard to mouth at one point. It was literally as poor as you can get in Britain without being homeless at one point. If you have ever been there you will never, ever take for granted that you don't need to worry. Never. I had a very very tiny baby and then I walked straight into poverty and depression. Clinical depression is a terrible place to be because it's not sadness. Sadness is not a bad thing. You know to cry and to feel, but it's cold absence of feeling. It's even the absence of hope that you can feel better. That really hollowed out feeling, that's what the dementors are. Poverty entails fear, stress and sometimes depression. It means a thousand petty humiliations and hardships. Climbing out of poverty by your own efforts, that is something on which to pride

> yourself. But poverty itself is romanticised only by fools. What I feared most for myself at your age was not poverty but failure.'

Despite fighting poverty and being rejected by 12 publishers, Rowling believed in herself and didn't give up. At 17, she was rejected from college. At 25, her mother passed away. At 26, she had a miscarriage, and at 28, she got divorced. When she was 29, she was living as a single mother, jobless and penniless, and at 30, she wanted to commit suicide. By the age of 31, she published her first book. In 2011, Forbes estimated her net worth to be $1.15 billion, and later on she donated a significant amount of money to charity. Her story just reminds us of how resilient she is and her attitude of never giving up.

In the Harry Potter books, Rowling discussed death and this is an inspiration for us as all because while we can't escape death, we should find our purpose before it comes for us.

Anna Akana, another of my favourite artists, shared her story of depression and how writing books and performing comedy helped her recover. In her book, *So Much I Want to Tell You,* Akana shares how she lost her teen sister to suicide and how she turned to stand-up comedy and YouTube as a form of creative expression. I started following her on YouTube and connected so well that I decided to perform improv comedy, which helped me feel so good as I was able to make people laugh. It was just like running an ultramarathon, though it is much more challenging to create a story out of nothing.

Mental health is a very big issue in the world right now and there is nothing wrong in sharing and doing something we love.

One of the most powerful female leaders in the world right now is none other than the Prime Minister of New Zealand, Jacinda Ardern. She is the second woman leader to give birth while in office, after Pakistan's Benazir Bhutto, and the first world leader to bring a baby to the U.N. General Assembly.

She was praised globally for her leadership after the Christchurch shooting in 2019. Although she has been criticised by some Kiwis over the country's slowing economic growth and plunging business confidence, she is one of the youngest world leaders to achieve remarkable things in her last two years of office, such as creating 92,000 jobs, 2,200 state houses, 140 million trees, better access to chemotherapy, cheaper doctor visits, taking mental health seriously, raising the minimum wage to $17.70, paying teachers, nurses and police officers more, banning semi-automatic assault rifles, introducing a zero carbon bill, lifting 50,000-70,000 people out of poverty and developing suicide prevention offices. Prime Minister Jacinda Ardern, while in office, has mentioned these achievements in a video message on her Facebook account: https://www.abc.net.au/news/2019-11-05/jacinda-ardern-facebook-speed-list-new-zealand-achievements/11671918.

What I am trying to say is that she has become a role model for millions of young women who aspire to be in positions of leadership. Very few know that she used to be a DJ in 2014.

Another politician I admire in United States is one of the youngest Congresswomen in American history, Alexandria Ocasio-Cortez. She used to work as a bartender at a restaurant in New York City's Union Square before taking up the role of Congresswoman.

She is an inspiration for many, as no human is limited. She is an example that one can still be in a position of leadership even if they come from a middle-class background.

Finland's Prime Minister, Sanna Marin, became the world's youngest leader at age 34. Not many people know that she used to be a cashier.

> 'My first job was a summer job at a packing company in a bakery in Pampere. In high school I distributed magazines for a while to get pocket money. After graduation, I spent the intervening years working as a cashier,' she wrote in her blog post in 2016.

She is a role model for many women out there, as even a cashier can become a Prime Minister and take up a position of leadership.

I also admire Canada's Prime Minister, Justin Trudeau, because he is a runner and often runs with North Atlantic Treaty Organisation (NATO) troops who have taken part in Canada's army runs. Such sportspersonship is welcomed in the world right now; we need world leaders to encourage sports as it helps us realise our full potential.

The power of never giving up and learning from our fears and failures are what we need in the world right now. When I read about people of influence and power and how they reached a certain height of success, it is only because they have courage and they never fear failure. Many people on this planet have failed before achieving success. There are no shortcuts to success, so we must learn from our failures and keep working hard. It is very important to not feel demoralised from failure, as there are millions of people out there to give you advice for free. I tell myself to ignore the nay-sayers and make my own choices.

When you suffer from failure, there is a big chance that you will give up on your dreams. When most people fail, they abandon their dreams and ambitions. Our lives are never going to be easy. They are like ultramarathon trails; there will be ups and downs, but we have to keep going. We might end up in bad relationships, we might end up in a bad career, we might suffer from a severe disease, but the only thing we can do is never give up and always have a fighting spirit. This is what number one world tennis champion, Novak Djokovic, teaches us. He came from Serbia, and when he was 12 years old, he witnessed war and innocent people being killed. He also had no tennis background and his family owned a restaurant business. What he taught us was how he, coming from a country that has experienced war, has transformed his feelings of revenge to resilience. Often, when we have bad experiences from people or a nation, we want to take revenge, but what if we turn this attitude in becoming the best version of ourselves and not giving up?

The story of David Goggins is also inspirational. He has been called one of the toughest men alive as it is believed he can achieve any task set before him. He came from a horrible background, where he was called derogative names all the time and had an abusive father. In his book, *Can't Hurt Me*, Goggins reveals how, despite some serious challenges in his life and recovering from a traumatic childhood, he transformed himself from being overweight to becoming one of the world's fittest soldiers. He ran one of the toughest ultramarathons in the world and inspired me to never give up.

All of us are facing some serious challenges in our lives. In fact, life is a challenge, but the most important thing is how we prepare ourselves for it.

Another influential woman is none other than Arianna Huffington. Her books *Thrive* and *Sleep Revolution* had a deep impact in my life, which is why I want to tell you her story. When she collapsed from sleep deprivation and exhaustion on 6 April 2006, she broke her cheekbone and got four stitches on her right eye. This was a wake-up call for her, as she then questioned the definition of success. By conventional means of success, which has two metrics: money and power, she was successful, but according to her, she was not successful if she was lying in a pool of her own blood on her office floor. So, she wrote *Thrive*, which talks about the importance of our wellbeing, wisdom, wonder, giving back and being kind. *Sleep Revolution* also created a significant impact in my life. As a runner, I know the importance of sleep. When I run long distances, I get a better sleep. So, Huffington's point is very clear; you have to do whatever it takes for you to recharge or refuel. For me, it is running ultramarathons, for you, it could be sleeping or baking.

Ellen DeGeneres is one of my favourite comedians, and the Ellen DeGeneres Show is one of the most watched TV programmes in the world. But let me tell you this: she didn't get successful overnight. I love her message of spreading kindness to make this world a better place. She often rewards people on her show who do something to make this world a better place. There is no place for jealousy, hatred or comparison in the world. We all our born to just be kind to one another. DeGeneres dropped out of university and did odd jobs such as painting houses, being a, vacuum salesperson and a waitress before she finally started performing as a comedian and got her big break on the ABC sitcom, Ellen. Her journey was not easy and she is a resilient women who never gave up despite the challenges around her.

I often try to investigate how we can share this attitude of never giving up.

Kunal Nayyar, known for the American sitcom *The Big Bang Theory*, is someone I also admire after reading his book, *Yes, My Accent Is Real*. I felt inspired by his journey to success and how he overcame failure in his life. He got his bachelor's degree in marketing and did his masters in theatre in the USA. His parents questioned his passion for acting, as it is a very difficult industry to break into, but he kept visualising his dreams, even after facing several rejections while only having 10 months left on his visa. He finally auditioned for a play and, after he got the part, moved to Los Angeles. He was living on a friend's couch and was working in a raw food restaurant. He also used to work at his university in addition to being a housekeeper. We often forget about the struggles people face when we see them achieving the heights of their success, but we all have to go through it and never give up. Kunal Nayyar's story is just an example for many that struggles are real, and we all have to go through them at some point in our lives.

One of the greatest cricketers of all time is none other than Sachin Tendulkar. He has been able to chase his dreams, and it took him 21 years to achieve one world cup for India. Tendulkar, in one of his speeches, said, 'Everything you achieve in life is temporary but what stays with you till the last breath is what kind of person you are.' This is so true, as when we die, nobody will remember us for our job status or what we contributed to the world, but for what kind of person we were and how we treated people around us.

> 'We all have been sent down by God with some talent, we just need to identify that and then from an uncut unpolished diamond to a priceless diamond, it is a process and the journey won't be easy. Don't give up and don't find short cuts. I think it is important to follow the right path always and in tough times tough people last.' Tendulkar added in one of his motivational speeches.

Tendulkar's journey was not easy, as he failed 10th grade. Yet, his parents were supportive of his wish to play cricket. Sadly, in India, sports are still not given much importance, other than cricket. Parents will not support a kid who wants to make a career in sports, movies or arts sectors. The mindset of my family was very similar; they never supported me, but after I wrote my first book, they eventually started feeling proud that I was doing some good work. I believe sports are essential in our day-to-day lives as they teach us valuable lessons like never giving up.

One motivational speaker, author and Bollywood actor I admire is Anupam Kher. He made it big in the film industry, with over 500 films to his name despite coming from a small town in Shimla, Himachal Pradesh, India. His dad worked as a clerk in the Department of Forest, and earned a mere salary of less than $2 a month when Kher was born. He is also one of my favourite motivational speakers. He grew up studying in a Hindi medium school and was often beaten by his teachers. He had been in over 150 films and was a very successful actor, but all of sudden, one day, he was diagnosed with facial paralysis. He could hardly speak, but in spite of doctors who told him to leave it everything for two months, he didn't stop working and played lighter roles, for which he had to speak less. Anupam Kher's story reminds us that we have to pass every test in life, though they may scare the hell out of us. He came from a very poor background but had big dreams. He was never good in studies and scored nothing more than 38 percent. He was also not good at sports and once his teacher told him, 'You will come second even if you run alone.'

There were four theatres in Shimla and Kher used to love watching movies. He knew he would not get any money from his father, so he stole Rs. 100/ $2 from his mother's house temple in order to go Chandigarh, a few hour's drive from Shimla, for his first audition. Finally, he confessed to his mother that he stole $2 in order to visit Chandigarh for his audition, and he was selected after the audition. When he visited Mumbai after rehearsing for six months for a movie, he was rejected as the leading man. But he fought his way back and didn't give up. Anupam Kher is one example of how, in this world, people can achieve greatness from nothing.

We are often told by people that we are too old or young for certain jobs. but trust me, no human is limited. There is no age to follow one's dreams, and remember, a lot of dreams are killed every day in this world because of family and societal pressures. It takes a lot of courage to follow one's dreams in spite of these pressures.

Morgan Freeman got his first big break in Hollywood at the age of 52. He is an example that it is never too late to achieve your dreams. We often give up on our dreams when we get rejected or fail. I was considered a failure until the age of 30, when I wrote my first book. Sometimes I feel that our families and the people around us become our enemies and do not support our dreams. If you have one true friend who has always believed in you and your dreams, please don't let them go away, because it is hard to find a friend like that. I am grateful for the opportunities I've had in my life, as millions of people in this world are suffering in this global pandemic of 2020. I am here to follow my dreams and not someone else's dream. Life is very short, but we can all make it meaningful one by following our dreams.

Eliud Kipchoge followed his dreams, too, and became the first human to finish a 42km marathon in under two hours. He is an example that no human is limited, if we try our best. He was raised by a single parent and always tried to convince himself to forget about his pain in marathons by focusing on the distance. In running, there is a saying that if you can convince your mind, you can achieve it. Telling our mind to not play games and to be positive is very important. Kipchoge always runs with his mind and heart, not just his legs. Mental fitness plays a very big role in competitions. Indeed, running marathons has taught me how to be mentally fit. Today, we need people with mental resilience. Today, we need mentally tough people who have the attitude of never giving up.

The story of Brazilian model Gisele Bundchen also inspires me to follow my dreams. Bundchen has appeared in almost 450 ad campaigns and on more than 1200 magazine covers. She has walked in nearly 500 fashion shows for some of the most influential brands in the world. Coming from a small town and making it big in the fashion industry was not easy, but she stayed resilient and strong.

Another great human, I got to meet is actor John Abraham. I got to meet him once, and trust me, Bollywood stars in India are worshipped like gods. What I like about Abraham is that he came from nowhere and made it big in the film industry. He had no godfather and worked hard to become one of India's top models before starring in films. He is a very down-to-Earth person and does not love showing off wealth, cars or other material things, which is very common in Bollywood. I really admire people who, despite of achieving so-called 'success' – money and fame – remain down-to-Earth and serve humanity.

Let me tell you Ed Sheeran's story. He was once homeless and spent three years sleeping on trains as he had nowhere to live. He started singing and playing guitar at the age of four, as his parents didn't want him to watch too much television and he was banned from playing video games. Though he was a creative genius, he didn't enjoy school and was bullied at age 15. A year later, he decided to quit school and follow his dream of making it in the music industry. His struggles grew, but he started performing in front of small groups and slowly he made it to the top charts on iTunes. He gained success after so many struggles and hardships. Many people give up on their dreams after failure or rejection, but some don't give up and just keep going. Ed Sheeran is just one example of this, and his song *Shape of You* is one of my favourites.

Kevin Hart is one of the most popular comedians in the world. His tours sell out football stadium and his films have collectively grossed over $3.5 billion. He reached such a height of success with so many challenges along the way, such as his father being a drug addict and his mother being overwhelmingly strict, beating him with belts and frying pans. Many people would give up because of these struggles, but Hart stayed resilient and laid out some significant lessons in his book, *I Can't Make This Up*. He describes how the construction of his life is still in progress:

> 'I am on a quest to find the ceiling of what's possible in this life and raise it, so that my children and their children and their children's children will look at my accomplishments and go, "holy shit." I am chasing after that holy shit effect.'

I guess this is a significant lesson for every human in this world who is chasing genius: if we don't believe in our own greatness, no one else will.

> 'You are limited only by your doubts, your fears and your desire to fit in rather than stand out. And there is room in this world for all of us to stand out.' Hart says.

Every one of us has to accept failure in order to succeed. There are no shortcuts, and no one in this world has succeeded alone. We need to build positive relationships with people around us in order to thrive and achieve greatness.

Hart's struggle reminds us about the pressure our families and society put on us to succeed. Sometimes, they don't understand that the path to success is through several rounds of failure. I come from India and I have seen through both my eyes and the lenses of Bollywood movies how much pressure Indian parents put on their children to succeed. They often love comparing their children to others and humiliate them when they fail, as though we were not born to fail but just to succeed. I wish I could teach them some of the valuable lessons I have learnt from failure. So many young people commit suicide around the world every day because of this pressure. Who should I blame – parents, family, friends, society, culture? One might argue that the people who commit suicide are not resilient and hold people's opinions into their heads for too long, but I am asking parents, workmates and society what right they have to treat people badly. Why can't we be kind to one another? As the Dalai Lama said, 'Our prime purpose in life is to help others and if we can't help them at least don't hurt them.'

Imagine if we were all taught this basic principle of life the day we were born into this world. To be honest, a lot of people are trying to bring change and preach wisdom, but we need a revolution; a revolution for kindness of spirit, for never giving up. We need a revolution to encourage people to follow their dreams and ignore the nay-sayers, we need a revolution of resilience, and finally, we need a running revolution to overcome all our challenges.

### Lessons Learnt From Trail Running and How I Connected to Nature

When I first came across trail running in Australia, I just got into the sport. The Surf Coast Century ultramarathon and the Delirious West 200 miler were some of the major trail running events I took part in. Thereafter, I started visiting Dandenong National Park in Melbourne every Sunday to train. The good thing about running on the trails and cliffs is that if you run in the mountains, running a marathon in the plains would look a joke to you. It makes us more mentally strong. Running, jogging or even hiking in the mountains is more difficult than running a marathon at the sea level. This helped me become more resilient and not give up easily during trail running. The biggest lesson I would say I learnt was connecting to nature and learning how to make meaningful human connections. We live in a rapidly changing world where we are often disconnected from nature. We are living in our own bubble, in air-conditioned offices, so we are not able to connect with nature. When I run ultramarathons, I am able to connect with my spiritual self and with nature. I often ask myself, how can I create a sustainable planet by running? Imagine the world without, or with fewer, cars, where people only run, walk or cycle to work and school. The world would be much better off, because climate change is real. Most marathons are won by Kenyans around the world. Have you ever wondered why? When I heard the story of Eliud Kipchoge, elite marathon runner, I came to know that children in Kenya run and walk miles to school due to a lack of transport facilities. As a result, running becomes a habit and a tough rural upbringing, simple diet, lack of junk food and running trails around the hills becomes a lifestyle for many.

According to author Adharanand Finn, in his book *Running With The Kenyans,* running offers a great chance for youths to make good money and transform their lives in the Kenyan community. The youth are surrounded by role models who have won medals across the world. These runners inspire the world with their amazing feats, and one of them is Eliud Kipchoge, who, as I said earlier, finished an official marathon in under two hours in 2019. I am pretty certain that these Kenyan runners are deeply connected to nature, as they train in the hilly trails. Nature sometimes gives us power to realise our full potential.

Today, we need more diverse and creative thinkers and spending time in nature helps us become more creative. I often ask myself, what is the purpose of my life? How can I contribute to this world and make it a better place? Is it by running ultramarathons, is it by writing books, or is it by giving motivational talks? I realised my purpose by running. I realised we have to change our thinking. As climate change activist Greta Thunberg said in her UN climate change conference:

> 'I care about climate justice and the living planet. Our civilisation is being sacrificed for the opportunity of a very small number of people to continue making enormous amounts of money. Our biosphere is being sacrificed so that rich people in countries like mine can live in luxury. It is the suffering of the many which pay for the luxuries of the few. The year 2078, I will celebrate my 75$^{th}$ birthday. If I have children maybe they will spend that day with me. Maybe they will ask me about you. Maybe they will ask why you didn't do anything while there still was time to act. You say you love your children above all else and yet you are stealing their future in front of their very eyes. Until you start focusing on what needs to be done rather than what is politically possible, there is no hope. We cannot solve a crisis without treating it as a crisis. We need to keep the fossil fuels in the ground, and we need to focus on equity. And if solutions within the system are so impossible to find, maybe we should change the system itself. We have not come here to beg world leaders to care. You have ignored us in the past and you will ignore us again. We have run out of excuses and we are running out of time. We have come here to let you know that change is coming, whether you like it or not. The real power belongs to the people.'

This was such a powerful speech by a then 15-year-old girl. Imagine how much courage and determination she has to change the world for good. We can all make this world a better place by having this kind of mindset. When I run marathons and ultramarathons, I meet leaders who think in a very similar manner. We need to teach people that running marathons in nature is cool, while driving or destroying nature in order to create jobs and make enormous amounts of money will eventually destroy our future.

Without a sustainable planet, we don't have a future. This reminds me of Hollywood actor Leonardo DiCaprio's speech at the United Nations climate summit 2014, when he said:

> 'Droughts are intensifying, our oceans are acidifying with methane plumes rising up the ocean floor. We are seeing extreme whether events, and the west Antarctic and Greenland ice sheets melting at unprecedented rates, decades ahead of scientific projections. None of this is rhetoric and none of it is hysteria. It is fact. The scientific community knows it, industry knows it, government knows it, even the united states military knows it. We need to put a price tag on carbon emissions and eliminate government subsidies for all oil, coal and gas companies. We need to end the free ride that industrial polluters have been given in the name of a free-market economy as the economy itself will die if our ecosystems collapse. Clean air and a livable climate are inalienable human rights and slowing this climate crisis is a question of our survival. It is time for world leaders to answer humankind's greatest challenge. We beg you to face it with courage and honesty.'

I always feel inspired by the above speeches, as they show leaders trying to make a difference. As a runner, I myself ask how I can connect to nature and make this planet a more livable one. If we change our lifestyles and our mindsets, lot of problems could be resolved. Each one of us are here to contribute in a way that can make a difference.

**Lessons From the Loss of My Mum**

My mum died in April 2002. To be precise, it was 2 April and I was around 12 years old. Losing my mum at such a young age was not a great experience, but it taught me some great lessons. The biggest lessons my mum taught me were to follow my dreams and respect women. She was an amazing cook, so I learnt cooking from her. She used to cook some of the best curries in the world. I enjoy cooking sometimes as well, but I am always afraid of gaining weight, so I try to cook them less. My mum wanted me to become a doctor and cure her of her illness; she was suffering from a severe disability called arthritis, where she had problems getting up and walking properly. She used to walk using a stand and often had trouble getting up from bed, so someone needed to lift her up. Her condition deteriorated and it was rare to find a cure at that time. I am so grateful I am in a healthy state today and am able to inspire people.

I was told I was born in a completely unhealthy state and was a very skinny child; I was underweight and malnourished. I remained skinny until the age of 17, but one summer holiday completely changed my look and appearance. I remember going for a summer break to my maternal uncle's house in Varanasi, India, from my boarding school Delhi Public School Mathura Road. That summer, I worked out in the gym twice a day for two months.

My maternal uncle, who also passed away few years ago, was a foodie. He loved food so much that he made me eat and I gained weight. As a result, when I returned from that summer break back to school, everyone started calling me 'muscle man.' Such a drastic transformation at age 18 was unbelievable for many and people asked me if I took any supplements or steroids, but I never took any in my life. As a result, I gained confidence and the people who bullied me in school started showing me some respect. I come from an educated family in India, where doctors and engineers were considered to be the most successful people. I chose none of these career options and became an ultramarathon runner and author.

If I can inspire one soul who has given up on life, then I consider myself as a doctor. Running has taught me so many important things and I only wish that, if my mum was still alive today, I could have motivated her to also live a meaningful life.

During these unprecedented times, I feel that running is important to keep us mentally fit and healthy. Every marathon I have ran in my life so far, and all the runs I will be doing in the future, are for my mum.

When I moved to Australia, I was feeling lonely all the time, so I made an Oz Mum. Her name was Sally Guilloux Cooke. She was one of my tutors at Monash University and was always there to guide and support me. She attended my graduation and my dad met her when he visited Australia. I remember she was trying so hard to get me a job after my graduation. Who does that for strangers in a foreign land? I considered her my Australian mother and used to visit her in her Williamstown house. She was a French woman who loved her red wine. In April 2020, I woke up to the shocking news that she had died of a heart attack. The world was already changing because of this Covid-19 pandemic and losing someone I was really close to was heartbreaking.

There is so much pain in this world. One day, you might get up and realise that you have lost the roof over your head due to a natural disaster like bushfires, earthquakes, cyclones or floods. One day, you could get up and realise that you have lost your job or a loved one. So, how do we stay resilient in these difficult times and never give up? Personally, running marathons and writing a book saved my life. For you, it could be any other hobby to refuel. Both of my mums, if they were alive today, would have been proud that I am following my dreams and inspiring people around me to not give up.

This pandemic, I would say, has taught us that life is short and there is no point of living someone else's life. Many people in this world are unhappy because they hate their jobs, are in a bad relationship or are in an unhealthy state. If we can get these three things right, we could be the happiest people on the planet. I would say my mum would be happy today because I am happy in my life and am doing well. I have achieved nothing in my life and also consider myself a failure, but when I look myself in the mirror every day, I say, 'no matter how bad life will be, I will never give up on my dreams.' Sports teach us so many lessons and today we need more marathon runners, more motivational speakers and more authors. We all have to die one day, but before we do, we should all leave a mark behind so that people remember us for our good work. I always try to become a better runner and a better author. Life is a beautiful journey and we all are here to learn from each other.

## Lessons from Being Disqualified from the Delirious West 200 Miles Challenge

I believe life is a lesson and a gift and every step we take teaches us how to live with purpose. Every failure is a journey towards success. Even I lose motivation after rejections and failures, whether it's a marathon or life in general. But every failure in my 31 years of life has taught me some significant lessons. Being disqualified from the Delirious West 220 Miles (350km) challenge was the lesson of a lifetime.

It is said that one should spend money on life experiences and not on material things, because while we might forget the things we buy, our life experiences will last forever. I was recently reading a book on Bhutan and came to know some interesting facts about it. For instance, in Bhutan, the government does not just measure the GDP (Gross Domestic Product) but also GNH (Gross National

Happiness). GNH is not measured by people's material possessions or whether they possess the latest iPhone, but by investigating whether people are involved in doing something they love or not. When I read this, I connected with it deeply, as when I run ultramarathons I live life to the fullest and I am one of the happiest people in the world. When I run, I am in my element and am able to connect with my spiritual self.

Recently, I connected with my spiritual side by running 204km in a 350km ultramarathon, or as I say, in an Australian *Survivor* challenge. This was not a normal ultramarathon but an extremely challenging course of event, and an effort to redefine the limits of human resilience. All 72 runners were expected to finish this extremely challenging course along the Bibbulmun Track, from Northcliffe to Albany in Western Australia, in 104 hours. Many humans would go crazy without sleeping for such a long time. I slept roughly 1.5 hours in the 52 hours of my run before I was disqualified at the 204km mark, the Peaceful Bay sleep station. I could give a million excuses for this failure, but I gracefully accepted it and promised myself to come back with better training.

Moreover, I realised that ultra-running events are community-building. They help us build lives, make lifelong friendships and give hope to millions of people in this world who have given up on life. I am very aware that millions of people live in extreme poverty, without proper food, electricity or water, and they suffer from mental illness. I was so grateful to be able to borrow some money from my friends and save for this event, as this was an expensive sport. Not everyone could afford it.

I don't take this for granted; I don't take my life, my food or my relationships for granted. When I am doing such extreme challenges, I am volunteering and giving back to this world by inspiring people to run, meditate, to do yoga and follow a hobby that can help them recover from stress and anxiety. As mentioned previously, suicide rates are high. Extreme poverty, bad relationships and bad health are some of the main reasons behind this. I am trying to make an effort to give hope to these people who have given up on life. Yes, life can be as tough as the Bibbulmun Track, but hope is the most powerful word in English dictionary. If we can run 350km on this deadly track, trust me, anything is possible!

The beautiful Bibbulmun Track was named after a subgroup of the Nyungar or Nyoongar people (Indigenous/first nation people), who lived in these lands for thousands of years, sharing the forest with birds, animals and rivers. They used to walk through these tracks as it consisted of surf coast, hills, trails and forest with snakes and other species of wildlife (Bibbulmun Track Foundation, 2020).

## Lessons From Relationships

There is no doubt that the quality of our lives depends on the quality of our relationships. There are many people in this world right now who are not happy because they don't have a great relationship, whether it is with their family, friends, work mates, housemates or partner. When we don't have great relationships, no matter how much money we make in life or whether we have a job title we are really proud of, there will always be some lack of fulfillment. Building relationships with people around us, especially during Covid-19 in 2020, is so important. I often feel lonely, although I have 1,600 friends on Facebook. Many of my friends say that social media has become a place to make comparisons and that there is much jealousy, hatred and negativity out there.

Our purpose of life is not to hate one another, but to love and be kind to one another. I am sure Covid-19 has taught us important lessons and the world won't be the same again. We don't need hatred or division in this world, but compassion for one another. We need unity in diversity. Life is not a rat -race my friend, it is a journey. Come, let's hold hands and go for a 100km and 200km run. We need to work together in order to become the best version of ourselves and reach greatness. Why are we here in this world? Each one of us has a gift and we are here to contribute to the world.

I am never happy when I don't have a good relationship with the people around me. I often get hate comments for running too much or even writing a book. But I tell my haters to please back off, because I will not stop running any time soon. In fact, there is a New York Times bestseller book called *Self-Help* by Miranda Sings, who also has a television series called *Haters, Back Off*. So, my point is, no matter what you do in life, there will always be someone around you who will hate you and you can't force every single person on this planet to like you. Even world leaders, celebrities and some of the most successful people on the planet get hate comments. The art is how you deal with it. Our lives are too short to make everyone happy. We need to love what we do and try to build positive relationships throughout the journey.

Great relationships and friendships are often built through sports. Growing up, I was never good at any sports, but I got into running after I ran my first marathon at age 20. When I run marathons, I build great relationships and make deep human connections. This is what we need in the world right now, when there is so much stress, anxiety, depression and loneliness. There is a saying that we make more human connections where there is no wi-fi. Every time I run in nature, I come across some great humans. Also, through running, I learnt the deepest lesson of my life: that the mind is an instrument and don't let it play it.

Running 100km or long distances is not difficult. The difficult part is to convince the mind that you can do it. Often, we make New Years' resolutions to go to the gym, to eat healthy or to have great relationships, but what happens is that we quit before achieving them. Many people start writing their book with full enthusiasm, but after finishing half of it, they quit, or they quit after being rejected by publishers. So, the hardest thing to do is convince the mind to write at least 1,000 words every day and set a strict deadline. Without a strict deadline, we would never finish writing our book.

I wish to someday write a book on relationships, though I am not a relationship expert. I know very well that my strong relationships are my secret to success. If I have just two friends who are always there to support me, cheer for me and feel joy when they see me achieve something, I don't need many friends. Your true friend is someone who is there for you when you have nothing to offer, because it's only when you become rich and famous and achieve so-called 'success' that the world wants to connect with you.

I would say that when I started building relationship with running, my relationships with my book and with movies became even greater. I realised I couldn't live without books and movies; they both have the ability to shift culture and change public opinion. I realised my father changed so much after reading my first book and as a result, my relationship with him improved. I received some positive comments on my first motivational book, which inspired me to write another. One of the biggest lessons I learnt was that sometimes we have to learn to live alone and find our purpose. Often, we get lost in this world and don't know what our purpose is. I know very well that the day I stop running, I will come closer to death. I love it so much – it is my fuel, my medicine. It helped me build a relationship with myself. Every day, when I get up, I ask myself if I am doing something I love. I ask myself, am I in the company of the person I really enjoy? I am not sure if I will be alive tomorrow because of the ways the world is changing. So, I am grateful that I have found my purpose at age 30 and that I have realised I am here to write books, run marathons, cook my favourite meals, sketch and paint, perform improv comedy and do everything that makes me feel alive.

My relationships and happiness levels are greater when I do what I love. Millions of poor labourers in this world have to work hard and do any job to survive, but I really recommend following a hobby once a week for people who are living a good life but are still not happy. I have been considered a failure my whole life, but the good thing about me is that I accept my failures and learn from them. If I hurt someone, I apologise and I make sure I treat them with respect. This helps me rebuild great relationships.

# Power of Resilience

### How Kindness and Compassion Helped me Recover from Stress and Anxiety

As a runner, I am very proud about how marathons and ultramarathons have taught me the importance of volunteering and how pursuing kindness and compassion in our daily rituals can enhance our wellbeing. Sharon Salzberg, in her book *The Force of Kindness: Change your Life with Love and Compassion*, explores the true meaning of kindness. According to her, kindness is truly a powerful force that can empower individuals and help them improve their relationships and eventually help them thrive in their environments, communities and ultimately the world. I would say that practicing kindness and compassion can help us become more resilient and recover from mental illness.

One of my favourite books, as I mentioned earlier, is *Thrive* by Arianna Huffington. In this book, Huffington lays out some significant lessons about giving and kindness. For instance, a small gesture of kindness every day can affect our mood, mind and body. You should also try to make personal connections with people we generally take for granted, like the checkout people at the supermarket, baristas, cleaners and uber drivers. If we try to communicate our hearts out with these people, we might be happier.

I never judge a person by their job, as a barista won't always be a barista and an uber driver won't always be a driver. Maybe they are struggling to make ends meet and will someday be the CEO of their own company, or maybe they like this work and it fits well in their life. So if we treat these people with respect and try to build a connection with them, we would be happier.

Another thing Huffington points out is that if we realise we have a skill or a gift and we can use that skill to educate or inspire others, we would eventually reconnect to the world. For instance, if I can run long distances like 100km or 200km and I use this skill to teach others who can't run even 200m, I am making someone else's life better while my own life is getting better.

I believe that compassion and kindness should be compulsory in every school and university in the world. We need to include these things in curriculums in order to make this world a better place.

Sometimes when I run a marathon, I ask myself, am I running for myself or for others? Will this running save lives, feed humanity, protect the planet and bring people together? How can I benefit humankind by running? If I can inspire one soul who has given up on life, it is worth running and writing a book. If I can raise money for charity for some great causes like mental health, cancer, HIV, or even the Covid-19 crisis, it is worth running a marathon. I love boasting on social media about my runs, but my purpose is to also serve humanity by inspiring others. If someone who suffers from depression or is a drug addict sees my post on running an 100km ultramarathon and decides to run a marathon, I feel like I have been successful in changing someone's life.

Mother Teresa was declared the pinnacle of human kindness. We need more people like her today to save this world. She dedicated her whole life to serving the poorest of the poor children in Kolkata and India and received a Nobel Peace Prize for her humanitarian work.

This also reminds me of Anand Kumar, who is known for his Super 30 programme in Patna, Bihar, India. He is a brilliant visionary and a book was written by Dr. Biju Mathew on Kumar's life journey, which was made into a Bollywood blockbuster. The Super 30 programme was based on changing the lives of 30 students from extremely poor backgrounds and educating them completely free of cost so that they could clear one of the toughest entrance exams in the Indian Institute of Technology (IIT). This culture of innovation was created by Anand Kumar with the goal that if you educate one person, you elevate an entire village from poverty and inequality.

I was so inspired by this book and movie.

Anand Kumar is an example of humanity and kindness. Imagine if we all started thinking of the underprivileged people of the world, who live in extremely poor conditions with absolutely no electricity, food or clean water. All of sudden, when a poor street vendor from Bihar who studied under street lights got a research position at a

European university, the global media took attention. This shows us that by serving humanity and being kind and compassionate to people in need, we can achieve greatness.

## Greatest Benefit to Humankind

Some groundbreaking research has proved that we are born for generosity and we all have some gift to serve humankind. A small act of kindness can enhance our wellbeing. According to a journal by American psychologists J.K. McNulty and F.D. Fincham, our relationships could improve and our wellbeing could be enhanced by four ostensibly positive processes: forgiveness, optimistic expectations, positive thoughts and kindness.

Buddhism also teaches us how we can be happier by practicing kindness and compassion. According to a scholarly research article titled 'Buddhist-Derived, Loving-Kindness and Compassion Meditation for the Treatment of Psychopathology: a Systematic Review', joy, equanimity, loving-kindness and compassion are four of our immeasurable attitudes.

The practice of compassion and kindness comes from the traditional Buddhist school of Mahayana. Buddhist practitioners who adopt and act upon such attitudes are known as Bodhisattvas. They practice selflessness and sacrifice to alleviate themselves from suffering. According to Buddhist studies, we are ignorant of the fact that being kind to one another and serving humanity leads us towards spirituality and alleviates us from all forms of suffering. According to Buddhist theory, if we practice compassion in our daily activities, we become more spiritually productive.

> 'You can never have an impact in the society if you have not changed yourself. I believe that in the end it is kindness and generous accommodation that are the catalysts for real change.' Nelson Mandela said.

I truly believe Mandela was a global leader who inspired us to chase humanity. He transformed South Africa with his unconditional love and kindness of spirit post-apartheid. Today, we need world leaders who preach about kindness and compassion. As the saying goes, the world is full of haters, so be an encourager first.

I am still investigating how a small act of kindness a day can change our lives. According to a social science journal article, 'Reactions To Random Acts Of Kindness', sometimes a small act of kindness is considered strange because it is not a societal norm and some people are skeptical. We have become selfish and we are not thinking of changing the lives of others in a positive way.

However, if we go by the 'Power of Kindness' scholarly journal by Obrien Anthony Kai Tiaki, Nursing New Zealand, acts of kindness by nurses help patients live longer.

An English dictionary meaning of kindness is to be considerate, benevolent, humane and helpful. We recognise acts of kindness when someone makes a sacrifice for others. Acts of kindness represent acts of generosity. According to the article, acts of kindness are not part of nursing curriculum, so these acts by a nurse is a reflection of care.

Why don't we encourage an act of kindness in every school curriculum in the world? This has the potential to make a big difference in someone else's life, and even our own life.

## Is Giving the Best Communication?

Are we born for generosity? Can a simple act of kindness help us make deep human connections? Can we find our purpose by helping others? Can it boost our confidence levels? Research by the Friends of Asia Foundation in Thailand tells us that committing kind acts not only helps others, but it also helps us feel better about ourselves. We don't have to become a philanthropist to think that we will donate to charity when we become rich. A small act of kindness, like helping a blind person cross the road, offering seats to women, children and the elderly on public transportation and offering to pay for someone in the supermarket who might be short of few cents or a dollar, can brighten up anyone's day.

In our every-day life we should always look for an opportunity to help others; this could involve making eye contact with someone or smiling at a barista. According to Sonja Lyubomirsky, a PhD professor at the University of California, 'People who engage in kind acts become happier over time. When you are kind to others, you feel good as a person – more moral, optimistic and positive.' It boosts our confidence levels. For instance, a feeling that we are abundant means we are able to give more.

Helping others boosts our physical and mental health. As American writer Robert Ingersoll said, 'We rise by lifting others'. Our mental and physical growth is directly related to how we treat people around us. According to Dr. David R. Hamilton, kindness creates emotional warmth, releasing a hormone known as oxytocin, which can reduce blood pressure and protect the heart. I believe that the act of giving releases this hormone, while the act of running releases endorphins, which makes us happy. There are many similarities.

Volunteering and giving back also helps us build lasting friendships and professional connections. As a result, we are happier when we have strong connections to people around us.

*'The best way to find yourself is to lose yourself in the service of others.'*
– Mahatma Gandhi

Mahatma Gandhi also taught some important lessons of kindness and humanity to the world. Gandhi dedicated his life to serving the people of India by gaining freedoms, improving living conditions and granting civil rights to his people. His principles of non-violence brought peace to the world. He gained respect and admiration for his belief in the service of others.

I am not asking you to become like Mahatma Gandhi or Mother Teresa, but we can be our own Gandhi; there is a leader inside us all and we can achieve greatness only by chasing humanity. The world is full of people chasing the two metrics of success: money and power. We have to create a trend where the youth are told to chase humanity from the beginning.

*'If I cannot do great things, I can do small things in a great way.'*
— Martin Luther King Jr.

One leader of the civil rights movement, Martin Luther King Jr., made an immeasurable impact in promoting non-violent protests and his message to spread kindness in this world made a huge difference.

*'No work is insignificant. All labour that uplifts humanity has dignity and importance and should be undertaken with painstaking excellence.'*
— Martin Luther King Jr.

These global leaders remind us that we are lacking a sense of humanity and today we need another set of leaders who will teach us to move in similar directions. The education system needs major reform. Most university graduates lack leadership skills. They are not being taught the importance of following one's dreams, the importance of chasing humanity or the importance of great relationships and true friendships. This is the biggest cause, despite the youth achieving so-called 'success', die of suicide. We need to dig into ancient books of wisdom that teach us about kindness and how it could help us recover from stress and anxiety.

There is a clear lack of culture, innovation and creativity in the education system today. To be honest, if I told my family that I wanted to become a poet, comedian or an ultramarathon runner, there is a chance I would be in big trouble. India is known for producing engineers. I wish the education system would have taught me how to live a meaningful life. Most of the world leaders I read about today didn't fit into the typical education trap; they always thought outside the box and created a revolution by educating themselves. I wish the education system today would have taught me how to survive in a jungle, where there are dangers like bushfires and snakes. I wish the education system taught me how to handle depression when I lost everything in a natural disaster, or how to control myself and my emotions like a world-class sportsperson. I wish the education system taught me that we all are born for generosity. I am not saying that the entire education system is corrupt or not showing us the right path – there are some really great education institutions in this world – but I am saying that we need strategies to build resilience.

**Joy of Giving**

According to a scholarly research article by Sara Konrath, 'The Joy of Giving', there are huge psychological benefits of giving. Research has proved that giving away our time and money makes us happier. Various studies have proved that there is a major correlation between volunteering and our wellbeing. Just like a drug trial, researchers once conducted a research on group of volunteers to analyse their mental health and wellbeing. After this group of people volunteered for a period of time, research proved that volunteering causes people to have higher self-esteem and feel less depressed. Being kind to others and treating people nicely around us also feels pretty good.

Further, the research shows that giving money to others, including charities, is associated with more happiness than spending it on oneself. The joy of giving research was conducted by asking participants to spend a small amount of money, say $5 or $10, on themselves versus another person, who spent that same money on someone else. The researchers tried to measure the participants' mood at the end of the day. People who spent their money on someone else were happier than those who spent it on themselves. Thus, there was a clear result that depicted the joy of giving and how any act of kindness or generosity changes our day for good. When we are happy, we are more mentally fit and healthy. The sad thing is that volunteering is still not encouraged in many parts of the world. I believe it should be compulsory in every school curriculum.

People who worked in corporate offices often felt that they were happier and their productivity increased when they donated money in specific contexts of the workplace. How often do you think people who chase the latest gadgets, like iPhones or iPads and branded clothes and bags, are actually happy for a long time? They often forget what they purchased after few weeks or months, but when they give money to others to make someone else lives better, it makes them feel richer. It is also proved that giving helps us recover from stress, anxiety and depression. These are some of the basic psychological disorders in today's world and only giving and having a kind attitude towards one another can help us overcome these challenges. The Covid-19 pandemic is a very challenging time for the world, as we are told to maintain social distancing, but I feel we need to ensure that we are connected to one another and volunteer as much as we can to save humanity. More people die in this world by suicide than Covid-19. I always think, I wish I could save the lives of people suffering from mental illness. We are told in this pandemic to maintain social distancing and to wash our hands, but the most important thing, which we often aren't told, is to build strong relationships with people around us or help someone who is really in need – like people with disabilities – follow a healthy routine and volunteer as much as we can.

The research has also proved that giving is associated with fewer symptoms of depression. Giving is contagious. Any act of generosity becomes contagious, as this inspires others, like close friends and family members, to do the same. Parents have a very important role in encouraging their children to follow giving behaviour; they have the ability to become a role model for their children by encouraging giving and kindness.

Research has proved that kind people in this world are more likeable. In any successful relationship, one partner always looks for kindness in another. In some ways, the secret to successful relationships is related to acts of kindness and giving; volunteering and donating money to charity helps us meet people with similar interests and build communities. People who volunteer have more social connections than those who don't. They also realise their importance by giving and escape the potential stresses of aging and declining health. There are also huge benefits to our physical health. For instance, research shows what happens to our brain when people make charitable donations.

Research by Sara Konrath shows us that when we donate money, the pleasure and reward centers of our brains light up as much as when we receive money. For instance, people who are highly kind, empathic and compassionate have lower levels of stress hormones after stressful events like natural disasters or the loss of loved ones. Volunteering is also associated with a lower risk cardiovascular disease. We all want a healthy and a happy life and several studies delineate that volunteering is associated with a 47 percent reduced risk of death.

Studies around the world have confirmed that volunteering is the secret to wellbeing in many cultures. Having money is important, as extreme poverty gives rise to mental illness, but if we are making $10 and giving away $1 to someone really in need, our life gets even better. Thus, being kind significantly improves our wellbeing.

According to leadership and career coach Emma Simpson, kindness makes us happier as we are rewarded with boost of the neurochemical dopamine, which makes us feel good about ourselves.

In the book, *Why Good Things Happen to Good People: How to Live a Longer, Healthier, Happier Life by the Simple Act of Giving* by Jill Neimark and Stephen G. Post we learn about astounding research about how we can enhance our physical and mental wellbeing by giving. Helping others can bring significant benefits to our health and help us recover from chronic illnesses, HIV, multiple sclerosis and heart problems. Volunteering, forgiveness and standing up for what we believe in also helps us.

I truly believe that there is a deep connection between generosity and personal wellbeing. We all practice wellbeing by eating healthily, running marathons and going to the gym, but we often forget the basic rule of mental fitness, which is kindness.

A study by Doug Oman, of the University of California in Berkeley, demonstrated that elderly people who regularly volunteered were 44 percent less likely to die over a five-year period. Studies have also shown that the secret to a lasting marriage is nothing but an act of kindness a day. No one today wants to marry a greedy, selfish person. In fact, researchers have argued that kindness is like a muscle that needs to be strengthened through repeated use. Just like we build our muscles in the gym, we need to also build a gym of kindness, which helps us build a habit of kindness. Once we get into the habit, we will always remember to practice throughout our lives.

I believe kindness is a religion that should be practiced in every part of the world. We need to restore faith in humanity by practicing kindness. Researchers have proved that too much media consumption often gives us stress, and as a result there is increased sadness and anxiety – especially during Covid-19. Today, we need more news on positivity, kindness and humanity.

According to Cindy Grimes, the spiritual leader of the OakBrook Center for Spiritual Living in Ocala, Florida, some of the benefits of kindness are increased oxytocin and serotonin, decreased blood pressure, less anxiety and depression and a longer, healthier life.

Her research further states that teenagers who practice kindness experience less depression and suicide, less involvement in risky behaviour, are less likely to fail in school, have increased self-esteem, greater social competence, remain happier and are more engaged. So, there are huge benefits from spreading kindness. Anyone can be kind, irrespective of race, color, religion or how much money one has. A simple smile, a kind word with a barista or a nice gesture can have a great impact on the life of another person. We need to be the change we want to see in this world.

*'Never doubt that a small group of thoughtful, committed citizens can change the world, indeed it's the only thing that ever has.'*
– Margaret Mead

According to the Dalai Lama's book, *The Art of Happiness*, excessive anxiety and hatred have devastating effects on the mind and body, becoming the source of much emotional suffering and even physical illness. However, we can recover from this phase by practicing kindness and compassion. As the Dalai Lama points out, a proper diet and exercise is essential, but we also need good mental hygiene, which is only possible by practicing gratitude and kindness. There should be no place for hatred in our lives. Buddhist practices encourage us to sow the seeds of full enlightenment – no matter how weak, poor or deprived one's present situation may be. Thus, if we can learn something from the Dalai Lama's teachings, we will all have the ability to make this world a better place by chasing humanity.

The Bible, too, says some great things about kindness and generosity.

*'Whoever is kind to the poor, lends to the lord, and he will reward them for what they have done.'*

*'The generous will themselves be blessed, for they share their food with the poor.'*

Even the *Bhagavad Gita*, which became a spiritual dictionary for Mahatma Gandhi, taught us about kindness and humanity. Gandhi was fascinated by two words from Bhagavad Gita: aparigraha (non-possession), which suggested renunciation on money and property to avoid cramping the life of the spirit; and samabhava (equality), which means to transcend pain or pleasure, victory or defeat, and to work without hope of success and fear of failure.

The Bhagavad Gita had a deep impact in the life of Mahatma Gandhi. Sometimes, we have to realise that we have nothing to lose and we are already naked. We will be a bigger loser the day we do not practice kindness; it is a weapon that makes us more resilient and mentally strong. If you ask me what strength is in today's world, whether it is showing off our guns and wealth or giving up our wealth for the service of others, I would say it is definitely the latter.

## Kindness is a Powerful Source of Resilience

Kindness is a powerful source of resilience. It teaches us stamina, passion and how to remain truly happy. According to a scholarly research article entitled 'How a Culture of Kindness Can Improve Employee Engagement and Patient Experience and Five Ways to Get There' by Shannon Landry, kindness is one of the most important factors when maintaining employee satisfaction. According to the research, kindness results in enhancing the productivity of nurses and hospital staff and helps them recover from burnout and stress. Nurses play a key role in driving a culture of kindness by engaging healthcare workers and other hospital staff. Both staff and patients, according to this research, are happier after practicing kindness.

## Kindness is Like a Marathon, Not a Sprint

From the above research, I conclude that kindness is like a marathon, not a sprint. We need to practice it for a very long time, like a never-ending ultramarathon trail. We often practice kindness and then leave it, but what if we are able to create a culture of kindness at home, at work, at school and everywhere we go? What if it becomes a daily ritual, just like brushing our teeth? In every marathon I ran, and every run I will go on in the future, I wish to practice kindness. It gives me instant energy, just like an energy gel or a sports drink. Kindness is another kind of energy. Maybe some are not visible. Just smiling at volunteers and giving them a high-five is an act of kindness. Many people ask me why I smile all the time. I tell them, 'I practice kindness.' Yes, even smiling is an act of kindness. You don't need to be a millionaire or billionaire to be able to practice kindness – we can do it on our everyday runs or while we are going for a walk – but the most important thing is to maintain it forever and not just for a small period of time. For instance, one day I earned $1,000 and decided to give $200 to people in my community who were in desperate need. I can repeat this every month, or once in a while, in order to recharge my brain for generosity. Just like I run marathons to recharge my mind, I also need to practice kindness to refuel myself.

**How to Build a Culture of Giving**

I think we need to build a culture of kindness and giving in order to live a meaningful life. I don't earn much at the moment, but it is my dream to build a culture of giving in this world in order to make it a better place. For instance, giving a smile or a hug costs nothing. According to the United Nations Sustainable Development Goals, more than 700 million people – or 10 percent of the world population – still live in extreme poverty in 2020. A large number of people live on less than $2 a day in Africa. The poverty rate in rural areas are much higher than in urban areas. 8 percent of employed workers lives in extreme poverty in 2018, which shows that having a job does not guarantee you a decent living. These figures show us the depth of one global problem, poverty, which leads to mental illness. So, this is the time to spread kindness and giving. We need to help and empower the poor and the needy. This is possible by creating a culture of giving. We need to let the world's most vulnerable people know that they are not alone and that humanity is still alive in this world.

## How Can I Solve One Global Problem by Running and Giving?

I have been running marathons for the last 10 years, but in 2019 I found my purpose by running long distances and ultramarathons. Every time I run, I ask myself, how can I make this world a better place by running? How can I create a running culture, a giving culture to solve global problems? There are thousands of global problems, but the biggest are depression and anxiety, which result from poverty and bad relationships. Various research by the UN has shown that many countries have reached their goals of economic development, but somehow lack human development. For instance, why are people still not happy even after they get rich? Why are suicide rates higher in wealthy countries? According to a scholarly research article by Vikram Patel, 'Poverty, Gender and Mental Health Promotion in a Global Society', 'the real wealth of a nation is its people and the purpose of development is to create an enabling environment for people to enjoy long, healthy and creative lives.'

The research says that our prime purpose in life is to be happy. Millions of people in this world are suffering from depression and anxiety disorders. This prevents them from carrying out their daily tasks effectively. As a result, it effects their sleep, and their wellbeing deteriorates. Many people struggle with substance abuse and excessive drinking, which further leads to other kinds of problems like domestic violence, suicide and mental illness. So, depression is a massive global problem, especially during Covid-19. I believe we can eradicate this problem not in a day, but over a period of time.

Firstly, as mentioned before, we need to engage in giving and kindness. We need to build strong relationships with people around us. We need to engage in doing what we love at least once a week. For me, it is running marathons, for you, it could be painting or music. We need to start meditating, practicing yoga and eating more green vegetables.

Stress and depression among individuals also result in economic slumps. Why is Bhutan called the happiest country in the world and other countries are not? Is the Human Development Index calculated by analysing whether or not people are engaged in giving or doing something they love? I often question these things while living in a first world country. Our end goal in life should be to chase happiness. Happiness could be money, power or strong relationships and doing something we love. Depression, drug abuse and suicide attempts, according to WHO, are some of the major challenges in front of us. These global problems have just two solutions: kindness and humanity. As the Dalai Lama said:

> 'The true essence of humankind is kindness. There are other qualities which come from education or knowledge, but it is essential, if one wishes to be a genuine human being and impart satisfying meaning to one's existence, to have a good heart.'

We can solve these global problems, which are a result of mental illness, with kindness. The recommendations put up by research scholar Vikram Patel brings to light how we need to improve access to healthcare and social welfare for people living in poverty, how we need to evaluate the impact of globalisation on mental health and how we can achieve sustainable economic development by uplifting marginalised people in society.

Every day, someone dies by suicide. Poor farmers in India commit suicide every day. In fact, a Bollywood movie called *Peepli Live* was made to bring notice to the problem of farmer suicides in India. Similarly, Indigenous people in Australia commit suicide and it never grabs headlines, but when a famous movie star or a businessperson ends their life, it becomes global news. I believe life is a gift and that we need to live our lives to the fullest. It can be challenging sometimes, just like a marathon, but I have seen lot of success stories, which are inspiring because anything is possible as long as we are alive.

## Kindest Country in the World

When I was reading about depression, stress and anxiety in 2020, I started investigating the root causes, such as why they are less prevalent in some countries and more common in others, and what the kindest country in the world is. When we are born, we should be told about two basic rules of life: kindness and giving. Is this possible? Are there any countries in this world that do this?

According to a study by the Charities Aid Foundation in 2017, one of the world's top 10 generous countries is Myanmar, formerly known as Burma. Its overall score was largely driven by its 91 percent donating money score. The country, which has a heavy Buddhist population, donates regularly to support the country's monks. The United States ranked second position, Australia third, and New Zealand fourth.

This study was based on following criteria: helping a stranger, donating money to charity and volunteering time to an organisation. While kindness is encouraged in some countries, others still lag behind.

It is difficult to say if generosity is more evident in developed countries than in those that are less developed. The most important thing we need is a culture of generosity in every country in the world. We need equality and kindness.

*'Only a life live for others is worth living'*
– Albert Einstein

## Some of the Poorest Countries in the World are Rich in Kindness

Some of the poorest countries in the world are rich in kindness. I started reading about these countries. I have friends from these countries as well, which helped me in understanding these countries better. Cambodia is one of the poorest countries in the world, but according to research scholar Elizabeth Nolan, it is a gentle land of kindness.

> 'Despite atrocities at the hands of Khmer Rouge, Cambodians smile ... they exude kindness. They routinely offer you what they have with no expectation in return. I have rarely come across people so hospitable, so friendly,' Elizabeth Nolan says in an article.

This just one example of a tourist's beautiful experience of kindness in Cambodia. Often, we hear so much negativity about some countries in the news and our perception of them changes. But when we visit those countries, we see the opposite to what we see on the news.

The Philippines is another country that is full of generosity. The country is full of warm, welcoming, hospitable and thoughtful people. I have been to Nepal once, and I guess the people there are very similar. Nepal is one of the poorest countries in the world, as far as their economy is concerned, but it is rich in heart and kindness. Thailand and Laos are similar. In fact, no country in this world is bad; it is the people who make it good or bad. There are negative people around the world who spread hatred and there are positive people around the globe who spread kindness, love and compassion.

According to some groundbreaking research and scientific findings by Harvard Medical School, when we take care of ourselves, we treat others better. So, kindness begins by being kind to yourself. And compassion can guide us to kindness. The research by Harvard Medical School reported that people's happiness levels boosted after observing kind acts for seven continuous days. Participants were randomly asked to be kind to strangers and themselves while observing their activities. The research says that we become kinder with practice. According to an ancient Greek storyteller, Aesop, 'No act of kindness, no matter how small is ever wasted.' Every kind act in our lives has a positive effect on our moods and wellbeing. One small act of kindness each day towards someone could be a game changer.

When I worked in customer service, giving a small compliment to a customer changed their day. For instance, if an alarm rang while a customer came, I told them that the machine beeped when a beautiful customer entered. Now these small, beautiful jokes can make someone's day. Who wants to be called ugly in this world? All of us want to look beautiful and be called beautiful. So, I generally try to compliment the people around me. This is just an example of a small act of kindness, which costs us no money. Such acts of kindness could have a lasting impact in someone's mind. As the saying goes: 'People will always forget what you gave them but will never forget how you made them feel.'

According to an article in the British Journal of General Practice titled 'Compassion and the Science of Kindness: Harvard Davis Lecture 2015' by Nigel Mathers, kindness is as an act of sympathy, distress, tolerance, empathy and non-judgement. Kindness cannot be faked. It is important in the healthcare profession, when caring for patients.

Ballatt and Campling's book, *Intelligent Kindness: Reforming the Culture of Healthcare*, talks about the impact of kindness on our brains. Any act of kindness by an individual releases endorphins (just like while running a marathon) and oxytocin, which makes us happy. Kindness can become a self-reinforcing habit, and as a result, it is the equivalent to going to the gym or exercising. The emotional and regulatory systems of our brain starts to activate by any act of compassion and kindness.

**Importance of Smiling**

Smiling could be interpreted differently in different cultures, but I believe a simple smile could be an act of generosity. According to an article in the Journal of Social Psychology titled 'The Effect of Smiling on Person Perception', by Sing Lau, a simple smile could make a person more likeable. Smiling increases our face value and gives a nice, warm feeling to others. It is an act of kindness.

A similar scholarly research article, 'The Effect of Smiling on Helping Behaviour: Smiling and Good Samaritan Behaviour' by Nicolas Gueguen & Marie-Agnes De Gail, says that a picture of a smiling face is more appealing than a sad face. Otta, Pereira, Delavati, Pimentel and Pires (1993) says that people who smile often are better leaders and are more optimistic, sincere and kind. A simple smile can increase the productivity of the smiling person. No matter how good or bad things are going, never forget to smile.

Another researcher reports that in restaurants and bars, waiters and waitresses get larger tips with a broad smile (Tidd and Lockard, 1978). A smile represents your helping behaviour and kindness.

Often, when we smile to a stranger, it enhances our helping behaviour. The findings from this research also show that smiling enhances the helping behaviours of people who are not smilers.

Ron Gutman, in his very fascinating TED Talk, talks about how to live a longer, healthier and happier life by smiling. While doing research with UC Berkeley's 30-year longitudinal study, he examined photos of students in an old yearbook and tried to measure their success and wellbeing throughout their life. By measuring the students smiles, researchers were able to predict how fulfilling and long-lasting a person's marriage would be. It also measured how inspiring the person would be to others.

Research by Wayne State University (2010) similarly looked at the baseball cards of major league players. The researchers found that a player's smile could actually predict the life span of the player. Players who didn't smile in the picture lived an average life of 72.9 years while players who smiled a lot lived an average life of around 80 years. We are all born to smile. Even babies in the womb can been seen smiling when we use ultrasound technology. Research says that children have the most amazing superpower of smiling, as they smile as much as 400 times a day. Being around a child or a pet also makes us smile more often. A study at Uppsala University in Sweden found that it is very difficult to frown when looking at someone who smile, because smiling is evolutionary contagious and it suppresses the control we have on our facial muscles. Charles Darwin also said that the act of smiling actually makes us feel better – it makes us healthier and reduces the level of stress enhancing hormones and increases our mood by enhancing hormones and reducing overall blood pressure.

*'I will never understand all the good that a simple smile can accomplish'*
*– Mother Teresa*

## Sports and Kindness

Sports also teach us to practice kindness. Sports keep the youth motivated and teaches us various life lessons. As a runner, when I lose faith in humanity, I run an ultramarathon and see some extraordinary humans who chase humanity and spread kindness through their talent.

## 10 Beautiful Moments in Sports

Sports teach us one important thing: to be kind, even to our opponent. Life is not a rat-race or a competition; it is a journey. We all want to win so that we get a trophy, but sometimes we need to uplift others in this journey as well. I can illustrate this with various examples. On every run I have done so far, I met someone who was struggling to finish the race and I gave them some motivation by saying: 'you got this.' Every time I have struggled, a stranger came up to support me. This is real sportsperson spirit.

We need to empower others in our journey towards victory. For instance, a soccer player carrying an injured opponent player to the pavilion is an act of kindness and humanity, and a tennis player helping their injured opponent and carrying them to the changeroom is an act of kindness. We all want to chase success and win prizes and money, but remember, we are all humans first. According to the Dalai Lama, our prime purpose in life is to help humans and if we can't, we have no right to hurt them.

Tennis legend Novak Djokovic once invited the ball boy, who was holding an umbrella behind him, to sit with him and have some juice while Novak took the umbrella from him. This act of kindness got millions of views on YouTube. We are often told that an apple a day keeps the doctor away, but the fact is that any act of kindness also keeps a doctor away. It leads us into a happier mood and our performance in sports or at work improves. A wrestler once carried his injured opponent to the changeroom for treatment. In every sport, we have observed an act of kindness by a player. This is an important lesson for all of us who are chasing success, money, power and medals. Those things are important, but kindness is even more important.

> *'It's nice to be important but it's more important to be nice'*
> – Roger Federer

## How to Build Resilience and Kindness

Building resilience through kindness is a very important tool in life and very few people know how to use it. To be honest, nobody really cares how much I can run, but people care about what I can do for them. How can I inspire them to run or follow their dreams? How can I educate them about the importance of kindness and volunteering? How can we all become more resilient and mentally fit by practicing kindness in our daily lives? These questions made me start doing some research on kindness and resilience.

I found this definition of resilience: 'The ability to become strong, healthy and successful again after something bad happens.'

We all have faced failure, setbacks and the loss of loved ones. There is so much pain in the world right now, when we are asked to stay resilient against the Covid-19 pandemic. In simpler words, we can only stay resilient by practicing kindness, and kindness spreads like water. According to a book by Bobbi Patterson, titled *Building Resilience Through Contemplative Practice*, a holy man was once asked how he could live a more resilient and joyful life. A Monk replied: 'I fall down and get up and fall down and get up.' Harvard professor Doris Sommer once said, 'Try again, fail again, fail better.' Often, we forget to fail in the race to chase success, but the truth is, we all have to fail again and again in order to become the best version of ourselves. We need to stay resilient and kind to one another. Another important lesson in Patterson's book is that when we let go of our breakdowns and move to the next chapter of kindness, we become more resilient.

By practicing selflessness and kindness in a world where there is so much greed, we all can become more resilient and build a community of love and compassion.

## Kindness Spreads Like Water

One virtue of kindness is what you can do for somebody else. How can you use your talent to make a difference in the lives of others? Just remember, people who are kind in a cruel world are true legends. Saying one kind word to another person could make someone's day. By commenting on people's on social media with phrases such as 'I love you', 'you are a legend' and 'I am proud of you', you are not just healing people, but performing acts of kindness.

Some people might feel insecure to see your achievements on social media, while others feel proud. We need five types of people around us: ones who inspire us, ones who celebrate our success, those who practice gratitude, those who help us grow and those who bring out the best in us (who help us become the best version of ourselves).

I always try to send a greeting card, flower or small gift to my close friends. It is an act of kindness and it helps us strengthen our friendship. I can proudly say that running has taught me to be compassionate towards strangers. A simple smile can make our day and help others who might be going through some bad life experiences. Someone might be hurt, lonely, in bad relationship, living in extreme poverty or suffering from a serious disease. So, a random act of kindness can help bring hope into the life of someone who has given up on life.

Simple words of encouragement include 'I believe in you', 'I am praying for you' and 'you look great today'. These words are acts of kindness. These acts of kindness can lift someone's spirits. Some people come into our lives to hurt us, while others come to heal us. Some teach us lessons, while others heal us from depression.

We often only see humanity rise in this world when we are in trouble. For instance, when a natural disaster strikes or a global pandemic like Covid-19 happens, what we need is an act of kindness. The United Nations took some initiative to spread kindness to the most vulnerable people in our communities. According to a United Nations staff member, a community in New York in March 2020 started implementing initiatives to help each other. Volunteers gave up their time to help senior citizens and disabled people and supplied food and water to people in need. Such acts of kindness shows us that humanity is still alive. We need more volunteers to help vulnerable people in some of the most difficult parts of the world.

Research by Stanford University, from the Centre for Compassion and Altruism Research and Education, says that kindness holds the power to heal. It means that the positive effects of kindness are even greater than those of drugs, or medicine like aspirin, and can reduce the risk of heart attacks. Often in hospitals, when patients are treated with kindness, they recover faster.

When patients recover from anxiety and pain, their wounds heal faster. Research shows that when doctors and nurses treat patients with compassion, patients are more likely to take their prescriptions and recover quicker.

According to Stanford University, 'Kindness is defined as a voluntary action undertaken with sensitivity to the needs or desire of another person and actively directed towards fostering their wellbeing or flourishing.'

The research further clarifies that when a patient is treated with kindness:

- They heal faster
- There is a 16 percent reduction in overall cold severity
- Diagnosis is more accurate
- They have lower blood pressure
- They are less likely to return to the emergency room
- They are more likely to listen to the doctor

So, any act of kindness in the healthcare system could be a game changer for the recovery of patients. Similarly, acts of kindness could also help us recover from mental illness.

**Be Human First**

Spreading kindness and compassion helps us recover from stress and anxiety. It also makes us realise that we all are in this world for a purpose, and that might be to chase humanity. Before we achieve anything, we should know the basic rules of life: kindness and humanity. I might become a millionaire or a billionaire by writing a bestseller, but there is no point of that success if I treat people around me with disrespect.

According to a research paper by Emma Seppala, from the Centre of Compassion and Altruism Research and Education at the Stanford University School of Medicine, and Kristin D. Neff, from the University of Texas, there are deep personal and interpersonal benefits of compassion. Their research points out some of the deep psychological health benefits of self-compassion and how it could help us build resilience and improve our relationships. Our wellbeing is determined by our ability to connect with and care for others. Compassion determines our quality of life at individual, interpersonal and societal levels. In other words, compassion is medicine for distress. Compassion involves elements of empathy, sympathy, altruism and selflessness. We also need self-kindness and self-compassion to recognise our failures and mistakes. Self-compassion helps us acknowledge our pain and gives us a mindful approach to problems.

There is so much pain in the world, but at the same time, practicing gratitude and compassion helps alleviate it.

Compassion also helps us understand ourselves and others better. It helps us live a fulfilling life. Compassion, and any act of kindness, is infectious. As the saying goes, 'a simple act of kindness creates an endless ripple.'

**How to Restore Faith in Humanity?**

In order to create a world full of kind people, we need to set up examples so that people can restore their faith in humanity. Often, we only see an act of kindness when only the world is in trouble, like in a pandemic, but the truth is, we all need to be kind to one another so that we can connect to the good person within us.

We all our born to be heroes to save lives in our field. Whether you are a doctor or a uber driver, we all have the ability to restore faith in humanity.

For example, a doctor saving the life of a patient and someone saving the life of a person at a beach who is drowning both display courageous acts of kindness and humanity.

Often, such people in our society do not get much recognition, but I believe they are true heroes. I remember when I was around 18 years old, I went for a trip to Goa, India, without telling my family. I almost drowned and someone saved my life. I was so grateful I survived and hugged the person who came to rescue me. I got a second chance at life as I was very close to death, struggling to breathe as I was trapped in the intense waves of the ocean.

I imagine that so many people die every day in road accidents or by getting trapped in some difficult circumstances. My heart breaks when I see people taking their own life. These people lose faith in humanity and they think that there is no one to rescue them. But when we come across extraordinary humans who are willing to sacrifice their lives for others, our faith in humanity is restored.

There are so many cases I often come across in the news, like the Tham Luang cave rescue, which is a brilliant example of restoring faith in humanity. The world came together to save the lives of a few innocent children who loved playing soccer. Unfortunately, there are so many cases happening on a daily basis that don't get enough media attention. We need to save lives on a daily basis and this is only possible by practicing compassion and kindness.

The Dalai Lama, in his Stanford speech, made some incredible points on how compassion and education can change our minds. I believe there are so many educated people in this world who go to expensive universities but treat people, like essential workers, with disrespect. For instance, a rich wealthy businessman treating a grocery worker or an uber driver with disrespect. Society often takes these people for granted, even though they work day and night to put food on their table. We need to be compassionate towards everyone, irrespective of their job status. This is true education.

The Dalai Lama points out that we need to change the minds of our opponents through dialogue, not force. We need to respect others who have different views. Youth have the responsibility of bringing compassion and peace to the 21$^{st}$ century and we need to train the youth to develop concern for the wellbeing of others. Indeed, peace of mind comes from warm-heartedness.

> 'I never consider myself as something special. If I consider myself as something different from you, like I am Buddhist, or even more, I am his Holiness the Dalai Lama, or even if I consider I am a Nobel Laureate, then actually you create yourself as a prisoner. I forget these things. I simply consider I am one of the seven billion human beings. We are mentally, emotionally, intellectually are the same.' The Dalai Lama said.

> 'The ultimate source of satisfaction is within ourself. If you do wrong things mainly harming others, You get negative consequences. If you help others and bring more happiness to others, you get benefits. You get more inner strength and more sort of confidence of purpose of life and fulfillment about that purpose, then you always feel happy,' the Dalai Lama added in his speech.

Today, we need more people like the Dalai Lama, who created a better world by spreading kindness and compassion. Humans are social animals, therefore friendship is essential for our survival. I still remember my two friends in Melbourne, who I often get in touch with whenever I am feeling low. They motivate me and I feel confident because they are always there for me. In this highly competitive world, we need strong relationships and true friendships. In the western world, people are so into technology, which makes us feel lonely. When I moved to Australia from India in 2016, I was feeling lonely all the time and I made books and running as my best friends. I started taking part in as many marathons as I could and read many books as well. Finally, they helped me find my purpose: to inspire people who have given up on life. I knew it I could only do it by running marathons and writing a book.

The Dalai Lama also says that fear and trust are contradictory things and so we need true friendship, which can help us fight mental illness and depression and lead us to humanity. I was feeling a sense of competition around me as well, as I was not able to make friends with people from my own country. I realised there is intense competition, and everyone had come to this Indigenous land in search of gold. I knew from the beginning that I was going the wrong way if I also started chasing what all my friends were chasing. So, I started educating myself and the people around me that jealousy and hatred brings frustration, and that loneliness comes out of our own mental attitude. I started developing my relationships by meeting extraordinary humans, limitless humans, in my running journey. Finally, I wrote my first book and after being able to sell few copies, I felt motivated to write a second book on chasing humanity by running. I guess the biggest lesson here is that we all are born for something unique and special and that is to spread love, kindness and humanity.

# Chasing Art

When I was around seven or eight years old, I won a painting competition in India. I remember struggling with a stomach-ache after the competition. I was not even aware that I had won the first prize. My name was in the local newspaper and my parents were really proud about this piece of fame. When I moved to my School in Delhi (Delhi Public School, Mathura road) I took Fine Arts in Grade 12 and scored 91 percent. I remember being the only guy in my art class. My family didn't care about my art marks, as it was not considered a good career option in India or around the world. As the saying goes, 'art doesn't pay the bills.'

I never wanted to be an artist, but I always enjoyed it as a hobby. There was nothing wrong in pursuing it as a hobby. Most of us, as children, have painted, but why do we lose our creativity when we grow up? Sometimes, our families do not support our pursual of art. I now ask all the parents around the world, who never support their children's talent, why? Today, art has immense benefits and helps us recover from mental illnesses, such as depression, and it also helps children with autism. Art, just like improv comedy, teaches us to be creative and helps us see the world from a very different perspective. We don't have to become Picasso, but just playing with some colours once a week or once a month can help us recover from modern-day stress.

## Art Therapy and Mental Health/Depression

According to a research article by Stanford Medicine, titled 'Creative Expression Improving the Quality of your Life with Art, Music, Poetry and Humour', creative expressions in the form of art helps improve our mental health. According to researchers Cynthia D. Perlis, B.A. Ernest H. Rosenbaum and M.D. Isadora R. Rosenbaum, art can be a healing force in our lives, and can help us express ourselves visually when we are unable to express verbally. Art also alleviate our moods and helps us out of depression.

According to this research, art has the ability to act as a medicine for elderly patients suffering from cancer. It also helps us realise our self-worth. Many people in this world do not try art because they are too afraid to be judged by someone. We don't have to be professional artists, but as long as we can play with some colours and sketch with pencils, we can feel good about ourselves. Imagine creating something new every day from our imagination. How good would we feel? Steve Jobs was also an artist in some way; he created products like the iPhone, Apple Watch and iPad, which many of us use today. So, we don't have to be professional artists, but experimenting with brushes can open up a wide range of ideas.

There is no age limit to use art to express ourselves. Creating art provides us with the ability to make decisions. It helps us improve our self-esteem and creates ways to relate to others in meaningful ways. Just like art, music and literature can heal patients suffering from mental illness, or other severe diseases. Art has healing powers and can reduce boredom and help people recover from depression, according to research. All of these creative instincts have the ability to divert our minds from disease or illness and help us become more optimistic and communicate our feelings with family, friends and medical teams. It can improve our wellness and quality of life.

According to Stanford University, art therapy also helps patients recover from post-stroke depression. Art can also act as an activity to evoke feelings of accomplishment, resilience, excitement and self-confidence. It encourages us to have meaningful interactions with others.

Art also helps children find their purpose. According to a research article titled 'Importance of Art in Child Development' by Grace Hwang Lynch, art education strengthens children's problem solving and critical thinking skills, decision making and visual learning. Art also improves children's academic performances and helps them grow mentally.

Thus, the benefits of art are enormous as far as our mental health is concerned. It helps people from all walks of life and of any age become the best version of themselves. It helps them boost their confidence.

## Art Therapy and Autism

Art is also an important tool that can help manage autism. According to award-winning researcher and author, Donna Betts from George Washington University, art therapy has the ability to help children with autism express themselves by using clay or making paintings. It also acts as a tool to express feelings and thoughts. For children who have a history of trauma, art helps them shift through their traumatic experiences and express their thoughts, which they are not able to express verbally. It helps children overcome the communication challenge that is present in autism.

## Why Do We Need Creative Geniuses?

The benefit of creativity is immense. As Albert Einstein said, 'Everyone is a genius but if you judge a fish by its ability to climb a tree, it will think all its life that it is stupid.' So, we need more creative people in this world who think outside the box. Unfortunately, society, family, university and schools around the globe do not always allow us to be creative and think differently, but people who think differently change the world for better.

Motivational speaker and author Jay Shetty highlights some of the habits of creative geniuses and how they think differently. Some of the habits of creative geniuses are writing journals, reading books, creating opportunities to be more creative, self-awareness, changing their mindset, changing their situations and putting themselves in challenging situations. Research shows that 75 percent of people in this world are not living up to their creative potential. If all of us become creative geniuses, we will have more people like Mark Zuckerberg and Steve Jobs. Facebook and Apple, two of the biggest tech giants, changed the world and most of us use them today. Jeff Bezos, of Amazon, and Larry Page, of Google, also created tech giants that are also heavily used today. We are so dependent on these tech giants. They created something useful for others. If my book created a similar impact in somebody's life, I would feel so good about it. So, creativity in any form, whether it is in books, art, improv comedy or the internet, has the potential to make the world a better place. People can become happier and find their purpose.

According to author Elizabeth Gilbert, there is a massive risk involved in creativity as well. If one wants to make a career in a creative field, one should be ready to take risks before having any success and should not be afraid to fail. We should continue to do our piece, whatever that might be. If our job is to dance, play music, paint or write a book, we should always keep pursuing it.

According to a research article from the American Psychological Association, titled 'Creativity and Genius' by Simonton, D.K., creativity is highly desirable in high-tech industries. Every organisation today needs someone who is creative as well as genius. We need to make sure that schools and universities encourage creativity, as this is how we can become creative geniuses.

Creativity also teaches us to face life challenges. Today, the world is in a state of transition and we need more creative people – people who can solve global problems. In the times of Covid-19, people are facing life-threatening hardships and we can stay resilient only by being creative. Art is one way, while improv comedy, cooking, running and writing are all creative activities that can make us feel good about ourselves. Today, we need a culture of creativity and innovation, as well as problem solving skills in business schools and universities. The current education system lacks vision, understanding and potential. It does not train us to face life challenges. But creativity teaches us how to cope up with stress, depression and how to overcome disruptions in our lives.

*'The important thing is not to stop questioning. Curiosity has its own reason for existing.'*
– Albert Einstein

Albert Einstein, who changed the world with his theory of relativity, taught us how to be creative. If you see most of the innovative leaders in the world like Steve Jobs, Bill Gates, Jeff Bezos, Sundar Pichai and Mark Zuckerberg, they are not successful entrepreneurs; they are artists. They encourage creativity at the workplace, they encourage innovation and questioning and they are always curious. Today, we need to build a culture where such kinds of creativity are encouraged. We all have different skillsets but we need to think like an artist, or like a runner, to be able to succeed in life. We all are born creative geniuses, but sometimes our parents, school and society treat us like dummies. We all have the creative potential to reach our goals and contribute to this world. We all have problem solving and innovative skills – it is just a matter of realising them. We need to encourage chasing genius instead of just seeking the two metrics of success: money and power. There is nothing wrong in chasing money and power, but creativity and innovation lead to genius.

**How to Remain Artists Our Whole Lives**

*'Every child is an artist, the problem is to remain an artist, once they grow up.'*
– Pablo Picasso

These are some of the motivational quotes by Spanish artist Pablo Picasso. We all have a gift, which God or the universe has given us. It is just a matter of realising what it is. My biggest gift is running long distances and I wish to use this gift to inspire a soul who has given up on life. There is some kind of creativity within us all, it is just that we are not aware of it. Picasso made us realise that we all are born artists. Any job in the world we do today requires creativity and problem solving skills. We need to stay resilient during life's journeys. Life is incomplete if we are not able to find our purpose. We all are born for something unique and special and that is to chase our passion. All of us have painted or done some artwork as a child, but as we grow up, we lose our creativity as we chase money and other metrics of success. It is ok if art doesn't pay our bills, because we should never lose our creativity.

## What Art Teaches Us and its Significance

Art is often encouraged among children and there are some serious benefits to it. According to an article by Dr. Lawrence Shapiro, 'The Secret Language of Children', children use art as a bandage for psychological hurts and bruises. This research indicates that even children can suffer from depression and art is a platform for them to express themselves. Children are often able to communicate their feelings through art. So, art is just one platform for children to express themselves. It also helps us to express ourselves in a meaningful way. It helps us recover from stress and anxiety.

# All My Paintings and Sketches

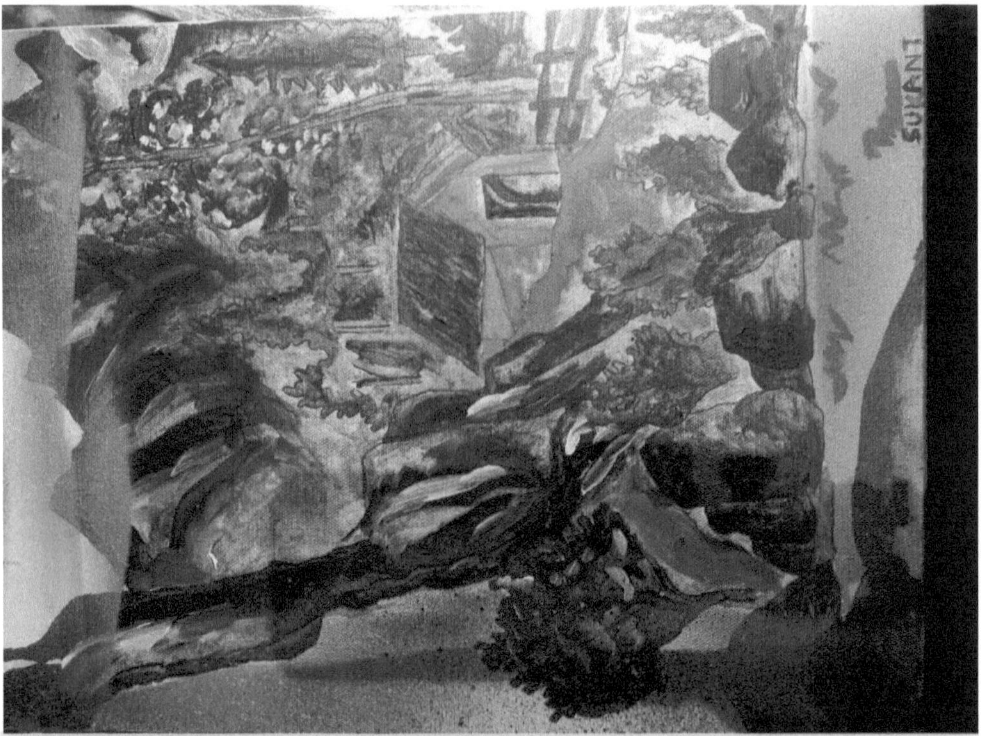
SUMANT

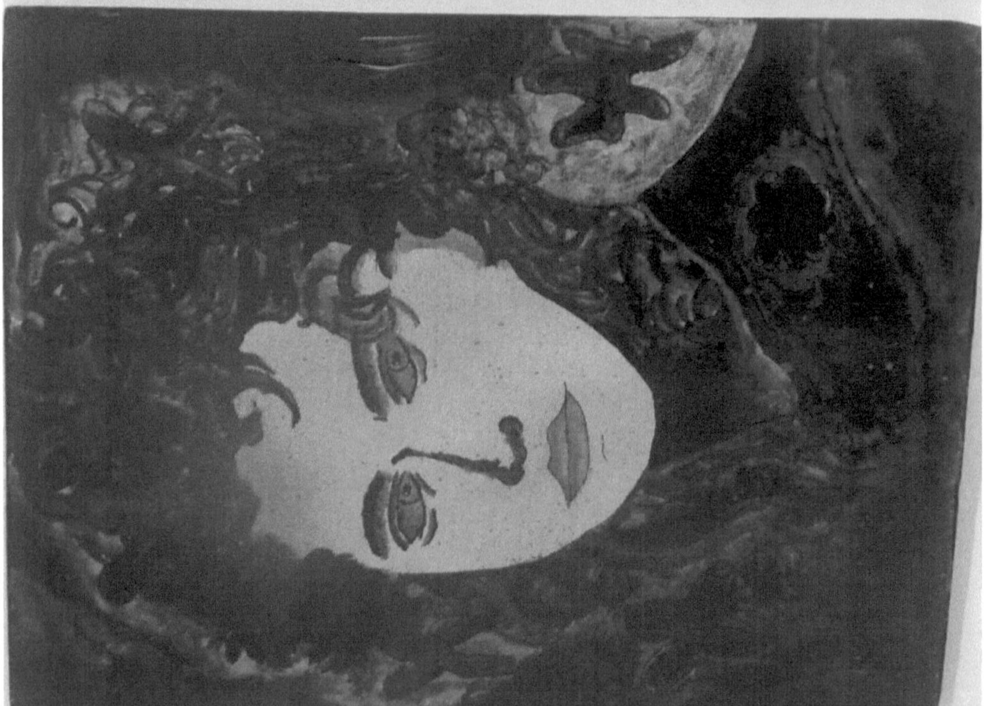

# Chasing Improv Comedy

Improv comedy is an art form. I was introduced to improv comedy by a friend and it was completely out of my comfort zone. I took it as a challenge, just like an ultramarathon. I believe that comfort is the thief of progress and if we are living in comfort, we can never progress. Life is all about trying new things that make our heart sing. Stepping out of our comfort zone to realise our full potential is what life is all about. We need to try everything, whether it scares us or not. I was never confident that I would be able to go on stage and make people laugh, but I did it after making several attempts. I failed my first attempt at level 1 improv, but I passed my second attempt and was so much more confident afterwards. Improv comedy is all about creativity; you create something out of nothing. It is not scripted, but the audience gives you a word and you create a story out of nothing with the help of other improvisers.

I was never surrounded with funny people in my life. In fact, I was told that doctors and engineers are the happiest people in the world. So, improv comedy was something very new to me. I wish this art form was introduced in every school and university curriculum. The lessons I learnt from improv are not taught by university, school, family or friends.

## The Lessons I Learnt from Improv Comedy

One of the most important lessons I learnt was how to fail and how to celebrate failure. We have all come to this world to achieve our dreams and succeed, but the path to success is through failure. Through improv, I learnt how to fail and everyone clapped when someone failed to perform an act. We celebrate our failure because it helps us learn.

If we could increase joy in our life and have a massive impact in the lives of others, why not? Some might say, 'We could have joy when we are surrounded by wealth, a big house, a big car, a private jet and material things' while others might say, 'we could enhance our joy with life experiences like travelling, running ultramarathons, painting, singing, sleeping, watching movies and reading books.' The fact is that we can enhance our joy by performing or watching improv comedy.

Galen Emanuele, in his TED Talk, says our perspective towards the world can change by being an improviser. If we use the principles of improv in our life, our life can change.

> 'Improv is about making other people look good, accepting ideas, being positive and saying "yes." When we choose to live a life with "yes", it changes the way we look at things,' Emanuele says.

Emanuele shares the story of a boy willing to run a marathon, but when he tells his dad, his dad responds in a negative way and questions his ability to run. As a result, the boy never runs the marathon. When I listened to this TED Talk, I connected with it so deeply. Several times in my life I have come across similar negative views. As a runner, everyone has questioned me when I told them I would run a 350km ultramarathon, a 100km ultra marathon or even 60km. But I just ignored the nay-sayers. Now, I just prefer to tell my two close friends who really believe in me. The biggest lesson of improv is that we need to uplift people around us and this is also an act of kindness. We can have a better marriage, better friendships and a better working environment as we become more positive through improvisation.

Another important lesson I learnt through improv are listening skills. Since childhood, I have been a very bad listener. Whether it was listening to teachers in school or to my friends, I could never focus when people used to talk to me. In improv, I learnt the importance of listening to monologues as I had to perform based on what was said.

Finally, the most important things of all are creativity and teamwork. Establishing base reality (who, what, where) in 30 seconds takes so much creativity. Based on a word given by the audience, and sometimes based on the monologue by one of the improvisers, we need to create a story. This improves our brain function and how quickly and positively we respond to our improv partners.

## How Improv Comedy Can Change the World

The question is: how can we make this world a better place by sharing the skills of improv? It is not every day that a child is born and their parents happily decide, 'Okay, let's make them a comedian.' In some conservative cultures, parents will never understand the importance of improv comedy in our human development. I joined improv not to become a comedian, but to learn certain life skills. Just like how running marathons taught me to how to survive in extreme situations, improv taught me to stay positive and smile even in dark times. We need to introduce this to the world as many people are not even aware of what improv is.

We can all create a better world by learning the art of improv; it is a life skill that teaches us how to be positive and accept things around us when the world is falling apart. Today, we need positive and optimistic people around us. The world is full of negative people and haters, so we need more optimism and encouragers. Every time someone has a big dream in this world, their society and families often try to tell them that their dreams are unachievable or impossible. But, as Nelson Mandela said, 'Everything seems impossible unless someone has done it.'

Improv comedy has the potential to create a positive culture in our society. It helps us grow individually as well as in a group. We can't live in this world alone; we all need someone and improv teaches us how to work in a team effectively and how to build relationships by making others look good.

According to a journal in creativity in mental health, titled: 'Improv to Improve: The Impact of Improvisational Theatre on Creativity, Acceptance and Psychological Wellbeing' by Diana

Schwenke, risk-taking in improv scenes helps us develop mutual trust in group work.

When one improviser supports another in a scene, risk-taking is rewarded. Risk-taking teaches us to overcome our fears and embrace new challenges. For people who suffer from mental illness or from personal loss, this improv exercise could help them develop trust in others and help them become more optimistic in life.

According to scholarly research, improv has the ability to enhance our psychological wellbeing so that we can become more accepting and creative. Our thinking also changes when we improvise. Most importantly, improv helps us develop a mindset that welcomes and embraces possible failures or shortcomings; we start developing a positive attitude towards self-respect and self-acceptance. Today, many organisations need creative thinkers who have problem solving abilities and great communication skills. Improv teaches us these skills. According to a study by Bermant, 2013 and Phillips Sheesley, 2016, improv helps us improve bodily awareness, mindfulness and psychotherapy.

Another great piece of research from The Journal of Creativity in Mental Health, titled 'Comedic Improv Therapy for the Treatment of Social Anxiety Disorder' by Alison Phillips Sheesley, Mark Pfeffer and Becca Barish, discusses how improv comedy leads to treatment of social-anxiety disorder. What is the definition of improv? According to this scholarly research, improv refers to any theatrical performance occurring without a script. It can be traced from commedia dell'arte in 15th century Italy to America in the late 1930s when Viola Spolin used it as a means of engaging children in community theater.

One of the improv exercises I learnt is to ask for a suggestion from the audience, which could be one word. According to this research, one of the most significant exercises of improv is to say 'yes' to other improvisers in order to build relationships among team members. Now, this is an important life lesson as it helps us build relationships with people around us. For instance, if one improviser starts by saying, 'Honey the room is dirty,' the second improviser could respond by saying, 'yes, honey, the room is dirty because I forgot to clean it.' Thus, each improviser responds by saying 'yes' and it eventually helps build a positive relationship. The research also says that the creation of fully developed scenes, characters and storylines in improv is a treatment for people who suffer from mental illness.

According to one improviser, Vicky Saye Henderson, improv comedy is active storytelling, or the art of possibility. In other words, it is the ability to create something that inspires the world. Improv teaches us awareness and how to take risks. We are able to establish the who, what and where by doing an act we don't always know the outcome of. So, we take risks and try to establish relationships with our partners in improv. It is like doing an act without knowing the outcome of the act. In order to have an approach in life, we don't just need to believe in our ideas – we also need have an open mind towards other ideas as well. This is an important lesson from improv.

It is said that we don't use enough of our brains in our daily activities. So, improv teaches us how to use a larger percentage of our imagination and use that imagination to create something so that it can make a difference in somebody's life. When I see audiences laughing, I build so much confidence.

Improv teaches us to embrace other people's ideas. One of the most important questions we need to ask ourselves is why are we here? Why are these people here and why right now? We need to be in the present moment and embrace other people's ideas. We need to make some great, simple choices that can get huge reactions from our audience.

Today, many organisations need employees who possess the basic skill of emotional intelligence. We need to make sure we are present in the moment and have active listening skills and engage with our team members. Improv teaches us how to live in the present and listen to other improvisers carefully. Being honest and truthful on stage also makes us look trustworthy. If we make a mistake, act nervous or laugh, we can share that with our audience so that they can enjoy it as well and accept our failure. Finally, rules of acceptance or agreement, as I mentioned before, always helps us be positive and build relations with other improvisers.

I personally believe that we live in a world where we are in a relationship crisis. We face confrontation on a daily basis with our bosses at work, our partner at home, our family members and even strangers on streets. Improv teaches us how to build relations with people around us. This is such an amazing lesson for the world and I feel that improv has the ability to shift cultures so that we have strong relationships. Bad relationships are one of the biggest causes of depression and loneliness in the west and if we can learn how to always remain positive and smile in even difficult circumstances, our life could get better.

## Why Should We be Chasing Improv Comedy to Recover from Stress and Anxiety?

Improv and mental health have deep relations. According to an article titled 'Can Improv Comedy Treat Social Anxiety?' published in *Psychology Today* by Jon Fortenbury, social anxiety is a very big challenge the western world is facing today. According to the National Institute of Mental Health, around 15 million Americans are suffering from it. Improv has certainly acted as a medicine for social anxiety. So, the big question is, how does improv have the ability to heal social anxiety? According to an improviser, David Alger, improv follows the rule of agreement, that is, saying 'yes' to other performers. This is why improv can be so helpful for social anxiety. Often, we suffer rejections from society, friends, family and workmates and suffer from anxiety. In my intro level 1 improv class, one basic rule we were taught was known as the 'failure bow.' This is where, when a student fails to perform an act, they bow and yell out 'I failed' and the other improvisers clap. This is called celebrating our failure. This is such an important life skill as we are often told that success is the most important thing, but without failure, there is no success. We need to learn to celebrate our failure, because when we accept our failure, we are less anxious about the future.

Improv comedy creates an opportunity for personal growth and exploration. In another article, 'Comedic Improv and Mental Health' by Ebony Ellis, group activities at improv like cohesiveness, exposure, humour and other healing elements could help in confronting social anxiety. Also, laughing in improv sessions has the ability to relieve stress, ease tension and improve one's mood. Improv also teaches us how to build trust and have conversations with strangers. When we learn to build good relations with people around us, our happiness level rises and our anxiety level goes down.

In the United Kingdom, students are often using improv classes to build their confidence, and most importantly, to get rid of their fear of failure. Improv teaches us one basic rule: there is nothing wrong to say. Sometimes, even if you say something stupid, you will hear the audience laughing. The audience is sometimes prepared to laugh and they just need something to make them do so. Improv teaches us to have a better link between our mouth and our brain. It helps us take decisions and react quickly to other improvisers. Another important life lesson I learnt from improv is how to accept a social invitation, or simply participate in a conversation. We learn to accept new ideas from our colleagues and friends and don't remain self-centred, that is, just thinking that our ideas are the best.

Nick Morgan, in his TED Talk, talks about the importance of laughter. It increases our oxygen intake, it stimulates our heart, lungs and muscles and it increases the endorphins released by the brain. The benefits of laughter are so wildly accepted that improv encourages us to laugh often. We live in such a stressful world and we sometimes forget to laugh. I personally forget to drink enough water, just like we forget to laugh and smile, without knowing how important it is for mental health. According to Nick Morgan, improv is an act of creating laughter with the help of other improvisers. Some of the core principles of improv are patience, kindness and humility. Mistakes are often referred as 'gifts' and they help us overcome our fears. We learn to honour the choice of our scene partners and try to look silly, leaving our pride at the doorstep. We learn to live in the moment and as a group we can conquer our fears. It also teaches us to build kindness, hope, trust and perseverance.

Some of the big corporate giants are using improv programmes today as part of their corporate training. McKinsey and Co. and PepsiCo are two examples. Improv is also an elective in many business schools, as improv principles are universal. If we approach creative problem with a 'yes' approach, there is no limit to how far an idea could be explored.

There are no limits to the experiences we can have in life with this 'yes' approach. Improv not only helps us cope with stress and anxiety, but it also teaches us how to live a meaningful life by facing our fears.

Most importantly, anxiety is caused by uncertain futures or fear of failure. For instance, one might be unsure if their job is secure, if their relationship is secure or if they will be alive tomorrow. If these thoughts are coming into our heads, it means we are suffering from anxiety. As an amateur improviser, I can say that I was taught not to base my scenes in the past or future but focus on developing the scene in the present and say 'yes' to my scene partner. Thus, improv teaches mindfulness, and mindfulness is nothing but living in the present. When we are mindful and living in the present, we can avoid anxiety and fear of failure in the future.

I failed level 1 as I had horrible listening skills. But later on, I started carefully observing what other improvisers had to say and I performed by using all the core principles. Trust me, it changed my life for good. I wish to do all six levels of improv one day and share my experiences with the world, so everyone knows how we can become more positive and recover from mental illness through improv.

**Laughter is the Best Medicine: Humour and Laughter can Influence Health**

We live in a very stressful world today and I can proudly say that chasing improv has taught me that laughter really is the best medicine. There is so much pain in the world, especially in 2020, and if we can make someone laugh in these difficult times, we are actually saving lives. I believe stand-up comedians and improvisers are in some way doctors who give patients laughter like it's medicine for pain. According to research by Professor Robin Dunbar at the University of Oxford, uncontrollable laughter releases chemicals called endorphins into the body and generates mild euphoria. The lungs empty as a result of these endorphin releases. The research by Dr. Dunbar points to the fact that the greater the increase in pain threshold due to laughter, the more endorphins are produced. The research also proved that laughter allows groups to bond, work better and act more generously towards each other.

According to David DiSalvo, author of the book, *What Makes Your Brain Happy and Why You Should do the Opposite*, there are six scientific reasons why laughter is the best medicine. Firstly, as mentioned before, laughter is a potent endorphin releaser. It helps build social bonds and boost brain connectivity, and is a key factor in strong relationships. It is a medicine for depression and it protects our heart. Research has proved that laughter has an anti-inflammatory effect and it protects blood vessels and heart muscles from the damaging effects of cardiovascular disease. Laughing is infectious, just like a smile, and spreading endorphin releases through groups promotes a sense of togetherness and safety.

'When someone starts laughing, others will laugh even if they are not sure what everyone is laughing about,' says DiSalvo. His interesting research points out how the quality of our relationships depends on how much men and women laugh. A study showed that women laugh about 126 percent more than their male counterparts, while men seem to instigate laughter the most. Couples who laugh more have greater relationships.

Research by California's Loma Linda University set two groups of people aside and asked one group to watch funny videos while the other sat silently. The saliva samples of the participants after 20 minutes revealed that the group who viewed funny videos had greater memory recall and decreased stress levels. Similar research by Vanderbilt University showed that just 10-15 minutes of laughter a day can burn up to 40 calories.

There are so many positive benefits of laughter in our life. The world is full of anxiety and uncertainty, but laughter can change your day. We become more positive and hopeful in life after a good laugh.

Laughter and love are the two most important tools, or medicine, for mental health in the 21$^{st}$ century. Music, dance and theatre are also tools that can help reduce anxiety.

According to a TED Talk by Dr. Rohini Rau in India, who is a certified medical clown, some hospitals have set up hospital clowns to cheer up patients. They are given proper training to deal with the hospital staff and patients.

Fabiola M. Mathew, in his research article, 'Laughter is the Best Medicine: The Value of Humour in Current Nursing Practice', laughter is a valuable human experience and is widely accepted to cure chronic ailments. Laughter is a great medicine for nurses as well as patients. It acts as therapy in many group situations and helps participants let go of feeling isolated, rejected, angry and fearful.

According to a research article by the American Journal of Nursing, 'Laughter is the Best Medicine: And it's a Great Adjunct in the Treatment of Patients with Cancer', nurses have the ability to bring joy into the life of patients. Things that might bring humour to the nurses and the patients include books, movies, sitcoms, comedy, cartoons and friends. Introducing humour into relationships with patients can uplift the spirit of the patient. The research says that while humour and laughter cannot cure cancer, they have the ability to alleviate fear, distress and anxiety.

Humour makes us happy and helps us cope up with adversity. Rhoda Weiss' article, 'Initiative Proves Laughter is the Best Medicine', shows us how hospital and healthcare organisations in California have initiated a number of humour-related programmes: for example, a 24-hour laughter channel based on comedy shows and entertainment and clowns visiting patients to make them feel better. 'Laughter helps tune up your immune system,' said Lee Berk, MD, assistant medical professor at the University of California.

According to The New York Times bestselling author Deepak Chopra, who has nearly written 90 books, laughter brings more joy into our life. Some of the key practices he recommends, which are centred on wellbeing, are: making humour a priority by reading a funny book, watching comedy, spending time with funny people, practicing laughter, yoga, focusing on finding a laughable moment of the day and telling a friend a funny story. These things can make us feel good.

Thus, we see that laughter can act like medicine, especially for patients suffering from severe diseases like cancer. My life completely changed by learning the art of improvisation. Laughing is one way to make this world a better place. As children, we laughed almost 150 times a day, but as adults, we often laugh less than 15 times a day or, if we have a bad day, not even that is possible. So, making laughter a daily routine could be a game changer.

## Do We Need More Comedians in this World? What is the Normal Reaction Parents Have When their Child Wants to be a Comedian?

We have seen that laughter is the best medicine and that chasing improv could help us learn innovative life skills and even help us cope with stress and anxiety. So, the next question is, do we need more comedians in this world? Do we need creative geniuses? Creating something out of nothing is a great talent and we need more of people who can do this today. Improv teaches us how to be healthy and live a meaningful life, but comedy is still not considered a lucrative career. In some countries, parents generally do not support their children to choose a career in this field. Having a sense of humour is said to be key to innovation, so there is nothing wrong in pursuing it as a passion or a hobby.

I have enjoyed each and every moment of my level 1 and 2 classes and wish to reach level 6 one day. Some of my favourite comedians around the world who have been successful in helping people laugh and forget their problems include: Jim Carrey, Jerry Seinfeld, Kevin Hart, Johnny Lever, Ellen DeGeneres and Trevor Noah.

These comedians have not only changed the world by chasing genius, but generated an immense amount of laughter that is otherwise missing in this world. Improv comedy is the need of the hour as it teaches us how to be more mindful and it also helps us make friends in the nature of games and exercises. It helps us realise that we should not take life so seriously sometimes. My listening skills have definitely improved with improv and it also helps us in being more creative. It helps us be less judgmental and helps our creativity flow. Improv also helps people build their confidence. It helps us interact with the world better. Improv is an art form where we make another person look good, so it also teaches us to be kind.

The benefits of improv are cosmic. Comedy is so essential for our physical and mental growth. According to the book *Laughing Matters: Understanding Comedy in Film, Television and Radio* by White G and Mundy, J, comedy is a significant aspect of contemporary culture and it helps us construct social values. Peter Perceval, in his TED Talk, makes the point of having funnier people in business. He says that if we can start a meeting by trying to make jokes, we can help generate new ideas.

According to a research by the Harvard Gazette, improv can boost the social and professional skills of students. Some of the greatest names in comedy, like Will Ferrell, Tina Fey, Amy Poehler, Chris Farley, Steve Carell and Stephen Colbert, started in improv.

According to this research, some of their great life skills like teamwork, collaboration, listening, communication and the ability to solve problems were learnt at improv. Helping one another is such an important tool at improv. If I said something that made no sense at all and no one supported me, I would look like a fool, so improv is nothing but an art to help each other and work in a team. Improv also teaches us to build social and interpersonal skills. We need to embrace diversity today and this helps us interact with people from all walks of life from various backgrounds and understand them, since we become more positive and accept more things.

To conclude, improv has the ability to change the world by changing our outlook towards life. We must become more positive and learn how to fail and celebrate our failures in order to succeed. Business schools have started teaching improv electives so that future entrepreneurs can use these skills in business as well as in life. Improv also helps us brainstorm. We learn that our ideas are important, but so are other people's ideas.

*My Improv Melbourne class Level 1*

# Giving Back

## Conclusion

At one point in 2020, I was feeling as though the world was coming to an end. With so many negative things going on, I was trying to find my purpose. I realised my purpose was to give hope to the 7 billion people on the planet and tell them that the world is a beautiful place, that life is precious and that we all have a special gift.

If I can have a purpose in life by running ultramarathons, doing improv comedy and painting, anyone can. Often, we think that we can only give back to the world when we become millionaires and billionaires. But the truth is, we can give hope to millions of people anytime. An act of generosity a day keeps the doctor away. We need to follow our dreams, treat people with respect and be kind to one another. These are the basic rules of life. I am not the best runner or author in the world, but every day I try to wake up with a purpose to give back by becoming the best version of myself. Maybe someday, I will run marathons around the world and raise money for various causes. Running and other hobbies helped me find my purpose. I forget all my problems when I run a marathon – I am in my element. If all of us find our purpose at some point in our lives, the world would be a better place. There is no doubt that the two metrics of success – money and power – are important in life, but we also need to chase genius, which, according to me, makes up the third metric: humanity, wellbeing, passion and purpose.

## Acknowledgements

After writing my first book, I didn't know how much the world read it but one thing I can say for sure is that my relationship with my dad (pitaji) improved so much that he started calling me a 'legend.' So, I decided to write my second book in the hope that my relationship with my dad gets even stronger. Every time I call him now, I say 'I love you.' He has done so much for me and I wish I can give back to him someday. I pray that he lives for 100 years because he is one incredible soul on this planet, and very few people can understand him. I also wish my mum was alive today to read my first and second book. I am very sure she is always watching me from heaven and I would not have been able to complete this book without her blessings.

I would like to thank the High Commissioner of India to Australia His Excellency A. Gitesh Sarma for endorsing my first book *Limitless Humans* and sending me a great letter of recommendation. It definitely motivated me to keep running and write my second book. I would also like to thank Louise De Domenico, adviser to Prime Minister of Australia, Scott Morrison for sending me a letter of encouragement on my first book.

Finally, I would like to thank my publishing guide, Blaise van Hecke, for her support. This is our second book together and I really appreciate her kindness and support through this process and helping me place this book in front of the world. Last but not the least, I would like to name and thank all the incredible athletes who participated in the Delirious West 200 Miler challenge in February

2020, as well as the volunteers, crews, pacers and organisers. Some of them created history by running 350km in a jungle and I got the opportunity to interview them. This book would have not been possible without their support.

Name of participants who finished the challenge: Jon Pendse, Elliot Eyers, Jimmy Brook, Guy Schweitzer, Mikko Kohonen, Glenn Monaghan, Sergio Gustinetti, Wayne Mcmurtrie, Dan King, Jiri Halek, Michal Cinciala, Chris Satherley, Brijmohan Sharma(Breeze), David Bennie, Glen Smetherham, Stephen Peacock, Matthew Salinovich, Georges Hombert, Markus Schar, Duc Do, Anthony Metcalfe, James Coffey, Aaron Crook, Reggie Howard, Sean Nakamura, Stuart Hopkins, Samuel Applegate, Scott Thomson, George Mihalakellis, Sarah Foster, Jen Millum, Melissa Robertson, Nicole Vaughan, Julie Brock, Natalie Reutter, Lauren Shay, Roylene Satnley, Cheryl Tatterton, Rebecca Brockwell, Lizelle Smith, Charmaine Brown, Aimee Brown, Kirsten Maplestone.

# Resources

Ernest H, Rosenbaum, M.D., Isadora R. Rosenbaum, M.A., Cynthia D. Perlis, B.A., John Fox, C.P.T., Malin Dollinger, M.D., Stu Silverstein, M. D., Jim Murdoch, 'Creative Expression Improving the Quality of Your Life with Art, Music, Poetry and Humour', https://med.stanford.edu/survivingcancer/coping-with-cancer/Creativity.html

Habits of Creative Geniuses, 'Think out loud with Jay Shetty', Huffington Post, https://www.youtube.com/watch?v=YlaA0FXbs_I

Simonton, D. K. (2008). Creativity and Genius. In O. P. John, R. W. Robins, & L. A. Pervin (Eds.), Handbook of Personality: Theory and Research (p. 679–698). The Guilford Press, American Psychological Association, https://psycnet.apa.org/record/2008-11667-027

https://haas.stanford.edu/students/cardinal-commitment/healing-strokes

http://www.enhancethearts.us/images/ChildDevelopment.pdf

Improv to be a Better Human Being: Galen Emanuele at TedxBellingham, Nov 22 2013, https://www.youtube.com/watch?v=VhkcmN-CCYw

Steitzer, Caitlin, Pages 270-282, The Brilliant Genius: Using Improv Comedy in Social Work Groups, https://www.tandfonline.com/doi/full/10.1080/01609513.2011.558830?scroll=top&needAccess=true

Alison Phillips Sheesley, Mark Pfeffer & Becca Barish, 'Comedic Improv Therapy for the Treatment of Social Anxiety Disorder', June 13, 2016, Journal of Creativity in Mental Health, https://www.tandfonline.com/doi/full/10.1080/15401383.2016.1182880

Jon, Fortenbury, 'Can Improv Comedy Treat Social Anxiety?' Psychology Today, https://www.psychologytoday.com/us/blog/neuroprogress/201508/can-improv-comedy-treat-social-anxiety

Ebony, Ellis, 'Comedic Improv and Mental Health, Free Spirit Media', https://freespiritmedia.org/features-search/2018/11/26/comedic-improv-and-mental-health

Rachael Healy, 'Improv Saved my Life: the Comedy Classes Helping People with Anxiety', The Guardian, https://www.theguardian.com/stage/2017/dec/20/comedy-improv-overcome-anxiety-depression

Pallab Ghosh, 'Study Reveals Laughter Really is the Best Medicine', BBC News, https://www.bbc.com/news/science-environment-14889165

David DiSalvo, 'Six Science Based Reasons Why Laughter is the Best Medicine', Forbes https://www.forbes.com/sites/daviddisalvo/2017/06/05/six-science-based-reasons-why-laughter-is-the-best-medicine/#31199a3a7f04

Yagana Shah, 'New Study Proves that Laughter Really is the Best Medicine', Huffington Post, https://www.huffingtonpost.com.au/entry/laughter-and-memory_n_5192086?ri18n=true

Fabiola,M. Mathew, 'Laughter is the Best Medicine: The Value of Humour in Current Nursing Practice', Nursing Journal of India, Vol. 94, July 2003, https://search.proquest.com/openview/ae1ff50554bce4a5eab83c355cf95261/1?pq-origsite=gscholar&cbl=35042

Tamara Lechner, '6 Reasons Why Laughter is the Best Medicine', Chopra, https://chopra.com/articles/6-reasons-why-laughter-is-the-best-medicine

Sense of Humour is the Key to Innovation: Peter Perceval at TEDxUHasselt, July 24 2014, https://www.youtube.com/watch?v=wLi143RYmD0

Juan,Siliezar, 'Improv Can Boost Social and Professional Skills, Students find', The Harvard Gazette, May 1, 2019, https://news.harvard.edu/gazette/story/2019/05/improv-skills-can-translate-to-social-and-professional-skills/

Edo, Shonin; William Van Gordon, Angelo Compare, Masood Zangeneh, Mark D. Griffiths, 'Buddhist-Derived Loving Kindness and Compassion Meditation for treatment of Psychopathology: a Systematic Review', https://link.springer.com/article/10.1007/s12671-014-0368-1

McNulty, J. K., & Fincham, F. D. (2012). Beyond Positive Psychology? Toward a Contextual View of Psychological Processes and Wellbeing. American Psychologist, 67 (2), 101–110, American Psychology Association, https://psycnet.apa.org/doiLanding?doi=10.1037%2Fa0024572

Kim, Baskerville; Kevin Johnson, Elizabeth Monk-Turner, Quita Slone, Helen Standley, Shannon Stansbury, 'Reactions to Random Acts of Kindness', The Social Science Journal, Volume 37, 2000- Issue 2, https://www.tandfonline.com/doi/full/10.1016/S0362-3319%2800%2900062-8?needAccess=true

Anthony O' Brien, 'The Power of Kindness', https://search.proquest.com/openview/92692ad4b4aa2a7b3faf0110b00d2799/1?pq-origsite=gscholar&cbl=856343

Random acts of Kindness Week: Volunteer in Thailand, 4 Ways that Helping Others can Enrich Your Life, The Friends for Asia Foundation, https://www.volunteerthailand.org/random-acts-of-kindness/

One Million Acts of Kindness, http://www.onemillionactsofkindness.com/2017/12/gandhi/

City of Kindness, http://cityofkindness.org/king-of-kindness/

Sara, Konrath, 'The Joy of Giving', 2016, https://scholarworks.iupui.edu/bitstream/handle/1805/10557/konrath_2016_joy_of_giving.pdf?sequence=1

Lars, Martin Fosse, 'The Bhagavad Gita', http://library.um.edu.mo/ebooks/b17771201.pdf

Linda Morrison, Colleen Cook, Kathy Bisson, Shannon Landry, 'How a Culture of Kindness can Improve Employee Engagement and Patient Experience and Five Ways to Get There', https://www.bluewaterhealth.ca/sites/default/files/2019-01/Cdn%20Nursing%20Journal%20Kindness.pdf

Sustainable development goals, 'End Poverty in all its Forms Everywhere', https://www.un.org/sustainabledevelopment/poverty/

Vikram Patel, 'Poverty, Gender and Mental Health Promotion in a Global Society', https://journals.sagepub.com/doi/pdf/10.1177/10253823050120020104x

Nolan, Elizabeth, International Forum of Teaching and studies, Marietta, Vol. 8, 'Cambodia a Gentle Land of Kindness', https://search.proquest.com/openview/379a51f8743f35642ded5670702b5cd0/1?pq-origsite=gscholar&cbl=38579

Melissa Brodrick, 'The heart and Science of Kindness', April 18, 2019, Harvard Health Publishing, Harvard Medical School, https://www.health.harvard.edu/blog/the-heart-and-science-of-kindness-2019041816447

Nigel Mathers, 'Compassion and the Science of Kindness: Harvard Davis Lecture 2015', British Journal of General Practice, https://www.ncbi.nlm.nih.gov/pmc/articles/PMC4917056/

Sing Lau, 'The Effect of Smiling on Person Perception', The Journal of Social Psychology, https://www.tandfonline.com/doi/pdf/10.1080/00224545.1982.9713408?needAccess=true

Nicolas Gueguen, Marie-Agnes De Gail, May 2009, 'The Effect of Smiling on Helping Behavior: Smiling and good Samaritan Behaviour', Vol 16, 2003, https://www.tandfonline.com/doi/pdf/10.1080/08934210309384496?needAccess=true

Ron Gutman, 'The Hidden Power of Smiling', May 11, 2011, TED Talk, https://www.youtube.com/watch?v=U9cGdRNMdQQ

Kathryn, Meisner, The ABCs of Resilience, TedxYMCA Academy, https://www.youtube.com/watch?v=bAHQJSKZDB0

Bobbi, Patterson, 'Building Resilience Through Contemplative practice', https://books.google.com.au/books?id=L7utDwAAQBAJ&pg=PT44&dq=stanford+university+kindness+and+resilience&hl=en&sa=X&ved=2ahUKEwjJ64qm7NrqAhVQyjgGHZ-wDjUQ6AEwAXoECAIQAg#v=onepage&q=stanford%20university%20kindness%20and%20resilience&f=false

'Acts of Kindness Spread Amid Covid-19 Outbreak as UN Acts to Counter Threat', Department of Global Communications, United Nations, https://www.un.org/en/coronavirus-disease-covid-19/acts-solidarity-spread-amid-covid-19-outbreak-un-continues-counter

James R. Doty, Lloyd Jean, 'The Healing Power of Kindness', Huffpost,
https://www.huffpost.com/entry/the-healing-power-of-kindness_b_6136272

Kristina D. Neff, Emma Seppala, 'Compassion, Wellbeing and the Hypo-Egoic Self',
http://ccare.stanford.edu/wp-content/uploads/2017/05/Neff-Seppala-chap-compassion-in-press.pdf

'Dalai Lama's Guide to Happiness', Oct 8, 2013,
https://www.youtube.com/watch?v=IUEkDc_LfKQ

Caroline, Praderio, Nov. 30, 2016, 'How Ellen DeGeneres went from unknown comic to talk show superstar',
https://www.insider.com/how-did-ellen-degeneres-become-famous-2016-11#she-left-university-of-new-orleans-after-one-semester-and-worked-odd-jobs-she-spent-time-as-a-house-painter-vacuum-salesperson-waitress-and-even-an-oyster-shucker-2

Sleep and Mental Health, Harvard Health Publishing, Harvard Medical School,
https://www.health.harvard.edu/newsletter_article/sleep-and-mental-health

# Also by Suki Singh

## Limitless Humans
*How Running Helped Me Live a Meaningful Life*

Available at all good online bookstores

Sukant Suki Singh is a runner. After running 22 marathons, including some ultramarathons, he has many lessons to share about how running has given him a deeper understanding of himself and the world.

In *Limitless Humans*, he tells how running the 100km Surf Coast Century ultra marathon changed his life and helped him to overcome stress and anxiety.

"One of the good things about this book is its timing. The pandemic has changed the world around us. It is for us to find meaning in life. The author has found happiness in running. Clearly, as the author has articulated, running is not only a test of physical endurance but also of mental strength and value of discipline. What makes this book special is that the writer brings out the universality of the running experience, having completed distances in iconic locations across the world. In the process, there were inspirational people to learn from, soak in nature's immense beauty and certainly value your own body, which we often take for granted. In the end, the book is exactly what it sets out to do, which is to pursue what you are passionate about."

— His Excellency A. Gitesh Sarma, Indian High Commissioner to Australia.

*nning 21 marathons and an ultramarathon is a remarkable achievement am sure your book will inspire other runners."*

– Louise De Domenico, Adviser to Prime Minister of Australia, Scott Morrison.

*"Suki is a young man of considerable substance and humanity who has written an inspiring story of courage and determination. In these difficult times globally, we can all learn something from his kindness of spirit and his admirable desire to change our world for the better."*

– Caron Dann, Lecturer, Monash University, School of Media, Film and Journalism and Author of The Occidentals.

www.ingramcontent.com/pod-product-compliance
Lightning Source LLC
Chambersburg PA
CBHW030256010526
44107CB00053B/1731